The
Flask Web Framework

Flask, PostgreSQL, and Bootstrap

Building Data-Driven Web Applications with CRUD Operations

MARK JOHN LADO

DEDICATION

To the dreamers who code and the coders who dream—this book is for you. Your relentless curiosity to transform abstract concepts into functional applications fuels the spirit of innovation that drives our digital world.

I owe immense gratitude to the open-source community, whose tireless efforts birthed tools like Flask, PostgreSQL, and Bootstrap. Your work democratizes technology, enabling developers of all backgrounds to craft solutions that matter. To the educators and mentors who selflessly share knowledge: thank you for lighting the way and nurturing the next generation of builders.

To my family, whose unwavering support carried me through late nights and early mornings—your patience and encouragement turned this vision into reality. To my colleagues and students, whose questions and challenges sharpened my understanding: this book is a testament to our shared journey of growth.

For every reader stepping into the world of web development: may these pages empower you to create fearlessly. Whether you're debugging a stubborn query or styling your first Bootstrap component, remember that every obstacle is a lesson in disguise. Celebrate progress, embrace iteration, and never underestimate the impact of your work.

This book is dedicated to the belief that code is not just syntax—it's a language of possibility. Keep building, keep learning, and keep inspiring.

— Mark John Lado

ACKNOWLEDGMENTS

Writing this book has been a journey filled with learning, collaboration, and inspiration, and it would not have been possible without the support and contributions of many individuals and communities.

First and foremost, I would like to express my deepest gratitude to the open-source community. Flask, PostgreSQL, Bootstrap, and the countless libraries and tools that make modern web development possible are the result of the hard work and dedication of developers around the world. Your commitment to creating accessible and powerful technologies has made it possible for developers like me to build and share knowledge.

A special thank you to my technical reviewers and beta readers, who provided invaluable feedback and insights throughout the writing process. Your attention to detail and constructive criticism helped shape this book into a more polished and practical resource.

To my colleagues and peers in the tech industry, thank you for the countless discussions, brainstorming sessions, and collaborative projects that have enriched my understanding of web development. Your expertise and willingness to share knowledge have been a constant source of inspiration.

I am also deeply grateful to my students, whose curiosity and enthusiasm have continually reminded me of the importance of clear and accessible teaching. Your questions and challenges have pushed me to think more deeply and explain concepts more effectively.

To my family and friends, thank you for your unwavering support and encouragement. Your patience during the long hours I spent writing, debugging, and revising this book has meant the world to me. Your belief in this project kept me going, even when the finish line seemed far away.

Finally, to the readers of this book—thank you for choosing to embark on this journey of learning and building. Your passion for technology and your desire to create meaningful applications are what drive the continued evolution of the web. I hope this book serves as a helpful guide and inspires you to explore, experiment, and innovate.

This book is a testament to the power of collaboration, community, and shared knowledge. Thank you all for being a part of this journey.

Table of Contents

This page is intentionally left blank.

Chapter 1

Setting Up the Development Environment

1.1 Installing Python and Required Libraries (Flask, psycopg2, Flask-WTF, etc.)

Let's delve into the step-by-step procedure for setting up the development environment, focusing on Python and essential libraries for Flask web development. Imagine building a system for managing student projects within a university. This involves handling sensitive data, complex relationships between students, faculty, and projects, demanding a robust and secure environment. The first crucial step is installing Python. It's generally best practice to download the official Python distribution from python.org (Python Software Foundation, n.d.). This ensures you have a clean and standard installation. Navigate to the downloads section and choose the appropriate installer for your operating system (Windows, macOS, or Linux). For production or academic projects, the latest stable release within the Python 3.x series is typically recommended. Avoid older Python 2.x versions, as they are largely deprecated. Once downloaded, run the installer. On Windows, ensure you check the box that says "Add Python to PATH" during installation. This allows you to run Python commands from your command prompt or PowerShell. On macOS and Linux, the installer usually handles this automatically. A common question arises: "Why not just use the system Python?" While some operating systems come with pre-installed Python, these versions might be outdated or configured differently, potentially causing compatibility issues. Using the official installer gives you more control.

After installing Python, open your terminal or command prompt. On Windows, you can search for "cmd" or "PowerShell" in the Start Menu. On macOS, use "Terminal" (found in Applications/Utilities). On Linux, the terminal application varies depending on your distribution. Now, let's install the necessary libraries. We'll use `pip`, the Python package installer, which is usually included with the Python installation. Type the following command and press Enter: `pip install Flask psycopg2 Flask-WTF`. This command fetches and installs Flask, the microframework for web development; `psycopg2`, the PostgreSQL database adapter, enabling your application to interact with the database (essential for storing and retrieving student and project data); and Flask-WTF, simplifying web form handling, crucial for students submitting project proposals or faculty managing project assignments. A frequent challenge is dealing with specific version requirements. Suppose a particular library requires a specific version of another. `pip` handles this. You can create a `requirements.txt` file listing all dependencies and their versions (e.g., `Flask>=2.0,<3.0`, `psycopg2==2.9.5`). Then, install all dependencies with `pip install -r requirements.txt`. This file is vital for reproducible environments. Another practical tip: If you're working on multiple projects with different library needs, use virtual environments. This isolates project dependencies, preventing conflicts. Use `python3 -m venv my_project_env` (replace `my_project_env` with your desired name) to create a virtual environment. Activate it using `source my_project_env/bin/activate` (Linux/macOS) or `my_project_env\Scripts\activate` (Windows). Now, install your project-specific libraries within the activated virtual environment. This ensures a clean and organized development workspace. By following these steps, you establish a solid foundation for building your Flask applications.

1.2 Setting up a Virtual Environment

Creating a virtual environment is a critical step in Python development, especially for projects like web applications built with Flask. Imagine you are developing two distinct applications: one for a library management system and another for an e-commerce platform. These projects might rely on different versions of the same library, say, Flask itself or a database connector. Without virtual environments, installing a newer version of a library for one project could inadvertently break the other. This is where virtual environments become indispensable. They provide isolated spaces for each project, ensuring that dependencies for one project don't interfere with those of another. The process begins after you've installed Python (as discussed in the previous section). Python 3 comes with a built-in module called venv (Python Packaging Authority, n.d.), which we'll use. Open your terminal or command prompt. Navigate to the directory where you want to create your project. For example, if you want to create your project in a folder called "library_app," you would navigate to that folder using the cd command (e.g., cd library_app). Now, to create the virtual environment, use the following command: python3 -m venv .venv. This command tells Python to use the venv module to create a virtual environment in a folder named ".venv" within your current directory. The dot before "venv" makes it a hidden directory on Linux/macOS systems, which is a common convention. On Windows, the command would be similar: py -3 -m venv .venv.

A frequent question is: "Why create the virtual environment in a hidden directory?" While not strictly required, it's good practice. Hidden directories keep your project folder cleaner and prevent accidental modification of the virtual environment files. After creating the environment, you need to activate it. On Linux and macOS, use the following command: source .venv/bin/activate. On Windows, use: .venv\Scripts\activate. You'll notice that your command prompt changes, usually by prepending the name of the virtual environment (e.g., "(.venv)") to the prompt. This indicates that the virtual environment is active. Now, any libraries you install using pip will be installed within this virtual environment, isolated from your system's Python installation and other virtual environments. For example, you can now install Flask, psycopg2, and Flask-WTF using pip install Flask psycopg2 Flask-WTF. Another common question: "Do I need to activate the virtual environment every time I work on the project?" Yes, absolutely. The virtual environment is only active when you explicitly activate it. When you close your terminal or stop working on the project, the virtual environment is deactivated. When you return to the project, you need to activate it again. A helpful tip: Some IDEs (Integrated Development Environments) like PyCharm can automatically detect and activate virtual environments for you. This simplifies the workflow. By consistently using virtual environments, you ensure that your projects are isolated, reproducible, and free from dependency conflicts, leading to a smoother and more efficient development experience.

1.3 Installing and Configuring PostgreSQL

Setting up a robust database system is fundamental to any data-driven web application. For our Flask projects, PostgreSQL offers a powerful and reliable solution. Imagine you're developing a platform for managing scientific research data. This requires handling large datasets, complex relationships between experiments, researchers, and publications, demanding a database system capable of ensuring data integrity and efficient querying. PostgreSQL, known for its robustness and adherence to SQL standards (Stonebraker & Kemnitz, 1995), is an excellent choice. The installation process varies slightly depending on your operating system. For Linux distributions like Ubuntu or Debian, you can often use the system's package manager. A common command would be sudo apt-get install postgresql postgresql-contrib. This installs both the PostgreSQL server and some helpful utilities. On macOS, installers are available from postgresql.org, or you can use package managers like Homebrew (brew install postgresql). For Windows, installers are also available on the official PostgreSQL website. During the installation, you'll be prompted to set a password for the postgres superuser. Remember this password; you'll need it later. A frequent question arises: "Why is there a postgres superuser?" This user has full privileges on the database server, allowing administrative tasks like creating databases and users. It's crucial to use this account cautiously and only for administrative purposes.

After installation, you'll want to create a new database and a dedicated user for your Flask application. This is a security best practice. Never use the postgres superuser for your application's database operations. On

Linux/macOS, you can typically access the PostgreSQL command-line interface using psql -U postgres. You'll be prompted for the postgres user's password. Once connected, create a new database using the following SQL command: CREATE DATABASE my_flask_db; (replace my_flask_db with your desired database name). Next, create a new user and grant them privileges on the database: CREATE USER my_flask_user WITH PASSWORD 'my_flask_password'; (replace with a strong password). GRANT ALL PRIVILEGES ON DATABASE my_flask_db TO my_flask_user;. These commands create a user named my_flask_user with a specific password and grant them all necessary permissions on the my_flask_db database. On Windows, you can use pgAdmin, a graphical tool for managing PostgreSQL databases, to perform these same actions. pgAdmin often simplifies database administration tasks, especially for those new to PostgreSQL. A common issue is forgetting the postgres user's password. If this happens, you'll need to consult the PostgreSQL documentation for your operating system on how to reset it. This usually involves modifying configuration files. Another practical tip: For production environments, consider configuring PostgreSQL for remote access (if needed) and setting up backups. These are crucial for ensuring data availability and security. By following these steps, you'll have a properly configured PostgreSQL database ready for your Flask application to use.

1.4 Creating a PostgreSQL Database and User for your application

Creating a dedicated PostgreSQL database and user for your Flask application is a crucial security and organizational step. Imagine you're developing a web application for a hospital's patient record system. This system will handle highly sensitive information, requiring robust security measures to protect patient privacy. Using a dedicated database and user for this application, separate from other applications or system processes, is paramount. This isolates the patient data and limits the potential impact of any security breaches. The process typically starts after you've installed PostgreSQL (as discussed in the previous section). You'll generally interact with PostgreSQL through the psql command-line tool or a graphical tool like pgAdmin. Let's outline the steps using psql. First, you'll need to connect to the PostgreSQL server using the postgres superuser account, which has full privileges. Open your terminal or command prompt and type psql -U postgres. You'll be prompted for the postgres user's password, which you set during the PostgreSQL installation. A common question is: "Why not just use the postgres user for everything?" Using the postgres user for your application's database operations is a significant security risk. If your application were compromised, an attacker would gain full access to all databases on the server. Therefore, creating a dedicated user with limited privileges is essential.

Once connected as the postgres user, you can create the database. Use the following SQL command: CREATE DATABASE my_flask_app_db; (replace my_flask_app_db with a descriptive name for your database, like hospital_records_db). This command creates a new, empty database. Next, create a new user specifically for your Flask application: CREATE USER my_flask_app_user WITH PASSWORD 'a_strong_password'; (replace my_flask_app_user with a descriptive username and a_strong_password with a complex and secure password).

Never use simple passwords in a production environment. A frequent question is: "What constitutes a strong password?" A strong password should be long, complex, and include a mix of uppercase and lowercase letters, numbers, and symbols. Avoid using easily guessable information like birthdays or1 common words. After creating the user, you need to grant them the necessary privileges on the database. Use the following command: GRANT ALL PRIVILEGES ON DATABASE my_flask_app_db TO my_flask_app_user;. This command grants the my_flask_app_user all necessary permissions (SELECT, INSERT, UPDATE, DELETE, etc.) on the my_flask_app_db database. A good practice is to grant only the minimum necessary privileges. If your application doesn't need to delete data, for example, don't grant the DELETE privilege. This further enhances security. Finally, you can disconnect from the postgres user by typing \q and pressing Enter. Your Flask application will now use the newly created my_flask_app_user and my_flask_app_db to connect to the database, ensuring a more secure and organized environment. This separation of concerns is a fundamental principle in database administration and application development.

1.5 Project Structure: Setting up your Flask project directory

A well-defined project structure is essential for maintainability and scalability in any software project, and Flask web applications are no exception. Imagine you're developing a complex web application for managing a university's research grants. This involves handling proposals, budgets, researcher profiles, and review processes. A disorganized project structure would quickly become unmanageable, making it difficult to find files, debug issues, and collaborate with other developers. A clear and consistent structure, on the other hand, streamlines the development process and makes the project easier to understand and extend. The first step is creating a root directory for your project. Let's call it research_grants_app. Inside this directory, we'll create several subdirectories to organize our code and other project assets. A common practice is to have a directory for your Python code, often named app or the same as your project name (e.g., research_grants_app). Inside this directory, you'll place your Flask application's core code. A crucial file within this directory is __init__.py. This file, even if empty, designates the directory as a Python package, allowing you to import modules and subpackages within it. This is a fundamental concept in Python packaging (Python Packaging Authority, n.d.).

Another important directory is templates. This directory will hold your HTML templates, which define the structure and layout of your web pages. Separating templates from your Python code makes your project more organized and allows designers to work on the front-end without needing to delve into the application's logic. Similarly, a static directory is used to store static files like CSS stylesheets, JavaScript files, and images. These files are served directly to the client's browser and don't involve any server-side processing. A common question is: "Why separate static files and templates?" This separation improves code organization and makes it easier to manage different aspects of your application. It also allows for more efficient serving of static files, as they can often be cached by the web server or a CDN. A requirements.txt file, as discussed previously, should also reside in the root directory. This file lists all the project's dependencies and their versions, making it easy to recreate the development environment on different machines. A good practice is to also include a .gitignore file in the root directory. This file specifies files and directories that Git should ignore when committing changes to the repository. This is crucial for excluding files like virtual environment directories, temporary files, and sensitive information. A frequent challenge is deciding how to structure more complex applications with multiple modules or blueprints. For larger projects, consider using blueprints to organize your Flask application into smaller, manageable units (Grinberg, 2018). Each blueprint can represent a specific part of your application (e.g., a user authentication blueprint, a data management blueprint). By following a well-defined project structure, you make your Flask applications more maintainable, scalable, and easier to collaborate on, ultimately leading to a more efficient and enjoyable development process.

1.6 Connecting Flask to PostgreSQL using `psycopg2`

Establishing a connection between your Flask application and your PostgreSQL database is a fundamental step in building dynamic web applications. Consider a scenario where you're developing an e-commerce platform. This platform needs to store product information, user accounts, orders, and other transactional data. PostgreSQL, with its robust features and ACID properties (Gray, 1978), is well-suited for such a task. However, your Flask application, written in Python, needs a way to communicate with this database. This is where psycopg2 comes in. psycopg2 is a powerful and efficient PostgreSQL adapter for Python, acting as the bridge between your Flask code and the PostgreSQL server. The process begins after you have installed both PostgreSQL and psycopg2 (using pip install psycopg2). Within your Flask application, you'll typically establish the connection within your application's code, often in a file where you initialize your Flask app. A common practice is to encapsulate the database connection logic within a function.

Let's outline the steps. First, import the psycopg2 library: import psycopg2. Then, define a function to establish the connection: def get_db_connection():. Inside this function, you'll use the psycopg2.connect() method. This method takes several arguments, including the database name, username, password, host, and port. These credentials are the same ones you configured when you created the database and user in PostgreSQL (as discussed previously). For example: conn = psycopg2.connect(dbname="my_flask_app_db", user="my_flask_app_user", password="a_strong_password", host="localhost", port="5432"). Replace these placeholders with your actual database credentials. A frequent question is: "Where should I store these database credentials?" Storing them directly in your code is generally discouraged, especially for production environments. A better approach is to use environment variables or a configuration file. This allows you to easily change the credentials without modifying your code. After establishing the connection, it's good practice to create a cursor object. The cursor allows you to execute SQL queries. cur = conn.cursor(). A common issue is handling potential connection errors. It's crucial to wrap the connection code in a try...except block to catch any exceptions that might occur. For example: try: conn = psycopg2.connect(...) except psycopg2.Error as e: print(f"Error connecting to database: {e}") return None. This prevents your application from crashing if the database is unavailable. Finally, return the connection object from the function: return conn. Now, in your Flask routes or other parts of your application, you can call this function to get a database connection: conn = get_db_connection(). Remember to close the connection when you're finished with it: conn.close(). A best practice is to use a context manager (with conn: ...) to ensure the connection is automatically closed, even if errors occur. By following these steps, you can securely and efficiently connect your Flask application to your PostgreSQL database, enabling you to store, retrieve, and manipulate data within your web application.

1.7 Introduction to Flask-WTF for form handling (if using forms)

Handling web forms efficiently and securely is a crucial aspect of web development. Imagine building a web application for managing student applications to a university. This involves collecting personal information, academic transcripts, letters of recommendation, and other sensitive data. Without proper form handling, you risk exposing this data to vulnerabilities like cross-site scripting (XSS) attacks or SQL injection. Flask-WTF, a Flask extension, simplifies the process of creating and managing web forms, providing features like form rendering, data validation, and CSRF protection. For Computer Engineering students and educators, understanding the intricacies of form handling and security is paramount. Flask-WTF builds upon the Werkzeug library for form handling and leverages WTForms for form field definitions. It provides a convenient way to define forms as Python classes, making your code more organized and maintainable. The process begins after installing Flask-WTF using pip: pip install Flask-WTF. Within your Flask application, you'll define your forms as classes that inherit from FlaskForm provided by Flask-WTF. Let's consider a simple example: a login form.

First, import the necessary classes from Flask-WTF: from flask_wtf import FlaskForm. Then, define your form class: class LoginForm(FlaskForm):. Inside the class, you'll define the form fields. For a login form, you might have a username and password field: username = StringField('Username', validators=[DataRequired()]), password = PasswordField('Password', validators=[DataRequired()]), submit = SubmitField('Log In'). StringField and PasswordField represent text input fields, while SubmitField represents the submit button. The validators argument allows you to specify validation rules for each field. DataRequired() ensures that the field is not empty. A common question is: "What other validators are available?" Flask-WTF provides a wide range of validators, including Email, Length, EqualTo, and custom validators. You can also create your own validators if needed. After defining the form class, you can use it in your Flask view function. First, create an instance of the form: form = LoginForm(). Then, in your template (HTML file), you can render the form fields using Jinja2 templating: {{ form.username.label }} {{ form.username }} {{ form.password.label }} {{ form.password }} {{ form.submit }}. Flask-WTF handles the rendering of the HTML elements for you. A frequent challenge is handling form submissions. In your Flask view function, you can check if the form has been submitted and if the data is valid: if form.validate_on_submit():. If the form is valid, you can access the submitted data through the form object: username = form.username.data, password = form.password.data. Flask-WTF also provides CSRF protection out of the box. CSRF (Cross-Site Request Forgery) attacks attempt to trick users into submitting unwanted data. Flask-WTF's CSRF protection adds a hidden token to your forms, which is validated on submission, preventing these attacks. You'll need to configure a secret key in your Flask app to enable CSRF protection: app.config['SECRET_KEY'] = 'a_secret_key'. By using Flask-WTF, you can simplify the process of creating and managing web forms, while also ensuring that your application is protected against common web vulnerabilities.

1.8 Integrating Bootstrap CSS: Downloading or using a CDN

Integrating Bootstrap CSS into your Flask web application is a crucial step for creating a modern and responsive user interface. Imagine developing a web application for managing a university's online courses. You need a consistent and visually appealing design that works seamlessly across different devices, from desktops to mobile phones. Bootstrap, a popular CSS framework, provides a collection of pre-styled components and a responsive grid system that simplifies the process of building such interfaces. It saves you from writing extensive CSS from scratch and ensures a consistent look and feel throughout your application. There are two primary ways to integrate Bootstrap: downloading the files directly or using a Content Delivery Network (CDN). Let's explore both approaches. Downloading Bootstrap involves going to the official Bootstrap website (getbootstrap.com) and downloading the compiled CSS and JavaScript files. You'll typically get a compressed archive (ZIP file) containing these files. After downloading, extract the archive to your project's static directory. A common practice is to create subdirectories within static to organize your CSS, JavaScript, and other static assets. For example, you might have a static/css directory for Bootstrap's CSS and a static/js directory for its JavaScript (and any other JavaScript files you might have). A frequent question is: "Why put static files in a separate directory?" Organizing static files in a dedicated directory improves project structure and makes it easier to manage these assets. It also allows your web server to efficiently serve these files.

Once you've placed the Bootstrap files in the appropriate directories, you can link them to your HTML templates. In your Jinja2 templates (used in Flask), you'll use the <link> tag to include the CSS file. For example: <link rel="stylesheet" href="{{ url_for('static', filename='css/bootstrap.min.css') }}">. The url_for('static', filename='...') function is a Flask helper function that generates the correct URL for your static files. This is important because the URL might change depending on your deployment environment. Using url_for ensures that the URLs are always correct. If you are using Bootstrap's JavaScript components (which often require jQuery), you'll also need to include those files. Place the Bootstrap JavaScript file (usually bootstrap.bundle.min.js or bootstrap.min.js) in your static/js directory and include it in your template just before the closing </body> tag: <script src="{{ url_for('static', filename='js/bootstrap.bundle.min.js') }}"></script>. A key consideration: Bootstrap's JavaScript components often depend on jQuery. If you're using these components, you'll also need to include jQuery. Download jQuery and place it in your static/js directory, including it before the Bootstrap JavaScript file. The CDN approach is simpler. Instead of downloading the files, you link to them directly from a CDN. A CDN is a network of servers that distribute static content, ensuring fast loading times for your users. Bootstrap provides CDN links on their website. You simply copy these links and paste them into your HTML templates, just like you would with the local files. For example: <link rel="stylesheet" href="https://cdn.jsdelivr.net/npm/bootstrap@5.3.0/dist/css/bootstrap.min.css">. A common question is: "Which approach should I use: downloading or CDN?" CDNs are generally preferred for production environments as they offer better performance due to caching. Downloading the files might be preferable during development when you're working offline or making modifications to the Bootstrap files. By integrating Bootstrap, either through downloading or a CDN, you can quickly and easily style your Flask web application, creating a professional and user-friendly interface.

Chapter 2

Defining Models and Database Migrations

2.1 Designing your database schema (e.g., for a simple product catalog, blog posts, or a to-do list). Choose a relatable example that you can carry through the entire tutorial.

Designing a database schema is a fundamental step in building any data-driven application. It's the blueprint for how your application will store and organize its data. For this discussion, let's consider a relatable example: a simple e-commerce product catalog. Imagine you're building an online store that sells various products. You need to store information about each product, such as its name, description, price, category, and images. This is where database schema design comes into play. A well-designed schema ensures data integrity, avoids redundancy, and allows for efficient querying and retrieval of information. For Computer Engineering students and educators, understanding the principles of database design is essential for developing robust and scalable applications. The process begins by identifying the entities you need to represent in your database. In our product catalog example, the primary entity is "Product." Other entities might include "Category," "Manufacturer," and "Customer" (if you want to track who is buying the products). A common question is: "How do I identify the entities?" Think about the real-world objects or concepts that your application needs to manage. These are often good candidates for entities.

Once you've identified the entities, you need to define the attributes (or properties) of each entity. For the "Product" entity, the attributes might include product_id (a unique identifier), name, description, price, category_id (a foreign key referencing the "Category" entity), manufacturer_id (a foreign key referencing the "Manufacturer" entity), and image_url. The product_id is typically an integer and serves as the primary key for the "Product" table. Primary keys uniquely identify each record in a table. A frequent question is: "Why do I need a primary key?" Primary keys are crucial for uniquely identifying records and establishing relationships between tables. They enforce data integrity and make it easier to retrieve specific records. The data type of each attribute is also important. name and description would be text fields, price would be a numeric type (e.g., decimal or float), and image_url would also be a text field. The category_id and manufacturer_id are foreign keys. Foreign keys are used to link records in one table to records in another table. They establish relationships between entities. In our example, a product belongs to a specific category and is made by a specific manufacturer. A common challenge is deciding on the appropriate data types. Choose data types that are appropriate for the data you'll be storing. For example, don't use a text field for a price if you'll be performing calculations on it; use a numeric type instead. After defining the entities and their attributes, you can represent them in a relational database schema. This involves creating tables for each entity and defining the columns (corresponding to the attributes) and their data types. You'll also need to define the primary keys and foreign keys to establish relationships between the tables. By carefully designing your database schema, you lay the foundation for a well-structured and efficient database that can support your Flask application's data needs.

2.2 Defining database models using SQLAlchemy (or another ORM if you prefer). Show how to define models with different data types (Integer, String, Date, Boolean, etc.) and relationships (one-to-many, many-to-many).

Defining database models using an Object-Relational Mapper (ORM) like SQLAlchemy is a crucial step in modern web development, especially when working with frameworks like Flask. Imagine you're building a content management system (CMS) for a blog. You'll need to represent data like blog posts, authors, tags, and comments. Directly interacting with SQL queries can be cumbersome and prone to errors. SQLAlchemy provides an abstraction layer, allowing you to interact with your database using Python objects and methods, making your code more readable, maintainable, and less susceptible to SQL injection vulnerabilities (OWASP, 2021). For Computer Engineering students and educators, understanding ORMs is vital for building efficient and secure applications. The process begins after installing SQLAlchemy: pip install SQLAlchemy. Within your Flask application, you'll define your database models as Python classes that inherit from db.Model (assuming you've initialized a db object using Flask-SQLAlchemy). Let's illustrate with our blog CMS example.

First, import the necessary classes from SQLAlchemy: from sqlalchemy import Column, Integer, String, Text, DateTime, Boolean, ForeignKey. Then, define your model class for blog posts: class Post(db.Model): __tablename__ = 'posts' id = Column(Integer, primary_key=True) title = Column(String(255), nullable=False) content

= Column(Text, nullable=False) created_at = Column(DateTime) is_published = Column(Boolean, default=False) author_id = Column(Integer, ForeignKey('authors.id')) author = db.relationship('Author', backref='posts') tags = db.relationship('Tag', secondary='post_tags', backref=db.backref('posts', lazy=True)). This defines a Post model with various data types: Integer for the id (primary key), String for the title, Text for the content, DateTime for the created_at timestamp, and Boolean for the is_published status. A frequent question is: "What are nullable=False and default=False?" nullable=False ensures that the column cannot be empty, enforcing data integrity. default=False sets a default value for the column if no value is provided. The author_id is a foreign key that establishes a one-to-many relationship between posts and authors. The author attribute allows you to access the author of a post directly, and backref='posts' creates a posts attribute on the Author model, allowing you to access all posts by an author. The tags attribute demonstrates a many-to-many relationship using an association table called post_tags. This allows a post to have multiple tags and a tag to be associated with multiple posts. The secondary argument specifies the association table.

Now, let's define the Author and Tag models: class Author(db.Model): __tablename__ = 'authors' id = Column(Integer, primary_key=True) name = Column(String(100), nullable=False) class Tag(db.Model): __tablename__ = 'tags' id = Column(Integer, primary_key=True) name = Column(String(50), nullable=False). And the association table for the many-to-many relationship: post_tags = db.Table('post_tags', db.Column('post_id', Integer, ForeignKey('posts.id')), db.Column('tag_id', Integer,

ForeignKey('tags.id'))). A common challenge is understanding relationships. One-to-many relationships are like a parent (Author) having multiple children (Posts). Many-to-many relationships are more complex, like students (Posts) enrolling in multiple courses (Tags) and courses having multiple students. By defining these models and relationships, you can easily interact with your database using Python objects. For example, you can create a new post like this: new_post = Post(title="My First Post", content="Hello World!", author=some_author, tags=[tag1, tag2]). SQLAlchemy handles the underlying SQL queries for you. This abstraction simplifies database interactions and makes your code more object-oriented and maintainable.

2.3 Introduction to Database Migrations (using Alembic or Flask-Migrate). Explain the importance of migrations and how to create and apply them. Practice creating migrations for your chosen model.

Database migrations are a critical aspect of managing the evolution of your database schema over time. Imagine you're developing a social media platform. Initially, you might have a simple user model with fields like username and email. Later, you might decide to add profile pictures, bio information, or other features that require changes to your database schema. Without database migrations, these changes can be disruptive and complex, potentially leading to data loss or inconsistencies. Migrations provide a structured way to apply these changes incrementally, ensuring a smooth and controlled evolution of your database. For Computer Engineering students and educators, understanding database migrations is essential for building and maintaining robust applications. We'll focus on using Flask-Migrate, which integrates Alembic, a powerful database migration tool, seamlessly with Flask. The process begins after installing Flask-Migrate: pip install Flask-Migrate. Within your Flask application, you'll initialize Flask-Migrate: from flask_migrate import Migrate; migrate = Migrate(app, db). This links Flask-Migrate to your Flask app instance (app) and your SQLAlchemy database instance (db). A frequent question is: "Why use migrations instead of just altering the database directly?" Directly altering the database can be risky, especially in production environments. Migrations provide a versioned history of schema changes, allowing you to easily roll back to a previous state if needed. They also make it easier to deploy database changes across different environments (development, testing, production).

After initializing Flask-Migrate, you can create your first migration. Run the command flask db init in your terminal. This creates a migrations directory in your project, which will contain the migration scripts. Then, create a migration script using flask db migrate -m "Initial migration". The -m flag allows you to provide a descriptive message for the migration. This command generates a Python script that defines the changes needed to create the tables based on your models (defined using SQLAlchemy, as discussed in the previous section). A common challenge is understanding the generated migration script. The script uses Alembic's migration language to define operations like creating tables, adding columns, and defining indexes. It's important to review the generated script to ensure it accurately reflects the intended changes. After creating the migration, you need to apply it to your database using flask db upgrade. This command executes the migration script, creating the necessary tables in your PostgreSQL database. As your application evolves and you make changes to your models, you'll need to create new migrations. Repeat the flask db migrate and flask db upgrade commands whenever you modify your models. A frequent question is: "How do I roll back a migration?" Flask-Migrate provides a flask db downgrade command to revert the most recent migration. You can also use flask db history and flask db stamp head to manage specific migrations. This allows you to easily revert to a previous database schema if necessary. By using Flask-Migrate, you can manage your database schema changes in a controlled and organized manner, ensuring data integrity and simplifying the deployment process. This is a crucial skill for any Computer Engineer working with data-driven web applications.

2.4 Creating tables in PostgreSQL using migrations.

Creating tables in PostgreSQL using migrations is the culmination of defining your models and setting up the migration framework. Imagine you're developing a learning management system (LMS) for a university. You've carefully designed your database schema, defining models for students, courses, instructors, and enrollments. Now, you need to translate these models into actual tables within your PostgreSQL database. Migrations provide the mechanism for doing this in a structured and manageable way. For Computer Engineering students and educators, understanding how migrations translate models into database tables is fundamental to building and deploying robust applications. The process assumes you've already defined your models using SQLAlchemy (or another ORM) and initialized Flask-Migrate, as discussed in previous sections. You've also created at least one migration script using flask db migrate -m "Initial migration". This script contains the instructions for creating the tables based on your models. The crucial step now is applying this migration to your PostgreSQL database.

Open your terminal or command prompt and navigate to your project directory. Ensure your Flask application's virtual environment is activated. Then, execute the command flask db upgrade. This command tells Flask-Migrate to apply all pending migrations to your database. Flask-Migrate checks the migration history table in your database to determine which migrations have already been applied and only applies the new ones. This ensures that migrations are applied in the correct order and prevents accidental re-application of the same migration. A common question is: "What happens if I modify my models after creating a migration but before applying it?" You'll need to create a new migration using flask db migrate -m "Updated models" to reflect the changes. Don't modify existing migration scripts directly. This can lead to inconsistencies and make it difficult to manage your database schema. Flask-Migrate compares your current models to the state of the database recorded in the migrations and generates a new migration script that captures the differences. Another frequent question is: "How can I see the SQL that will be executed by the migration?" You can use the flask db stamp head command to mark the current migration as applied without actually running it. Then, you can use a tool like pgAdmin or the psql command-line interface to inspect the database schema and see the changes that would be applied. This can be helpful for debugging and understanding the impact of your migrations.

After running flask db upgrade, your PostgreSQL database will now contain the tables corresponding to your SQLAlchemy models. You can connect to your database using psql or pgAdmin to verify that the tables have been created and that the columns have the correct data types and constraints. A common challenge is dealing with foreign key relationships. Flask-Migrate automatically handles the creation of foreign key constraints based on your model definitions. However, it's essential to understand how these relationships are represented in the database. Foreign keys ensure referential integrity, meaning that related records in different tables are consistent. For example, in our LMS, the enrollments table would have foreign keys referencing both the students and courses tables, ensuring that an enrollment record can only refer to existing students and courses. By using migrations to create your database tables, you ensure a consistent and reproducible process. This is crucial for managing database schema changes in a team environment and for deploying your application to different environments. Migrations provide a versioned history of your database schema, making it easier to track changes and roll back to previous versions if necessary.

Chapter 3

Creating (C)

3.1 Designing the "Create" form using Flask-WTF (or just plain HTML if keeping it simple). Include relevant input fields for your chosen model.

Designing a "Create" form is a fundamental step in building any web application that allows users to input and store data. Let's continue with our e-commerce product catalog example. We need a form that allows administrators to add new products to the catalog, including their name, description, price, category, and images. For Computer Engineering students and educators, understanding how to create effective and secure forms is crucial for building user-friendly and robust applications. We'll use Flask-WTF to simplify form creation and handling, providing built-in features for validation and security. The process begins after installing Flask-WTF (pip install Flask-WTF) and defining your product model using SQLAlchemy, as discussed in previous sections. You'll create a Python class that inherits from FlaskForm to represent your product creation form.

First, import the necessary classes from Flask-WTF: from flask_wtf import FlaskForm; from wtforms import StringField, TextAreaField, DecimalField, IntegerField, FileField, SubmitField; from wtforms.validators import DataRequired. Then, define your form class: class ProductForm(FlaskForm): name = StringField('Product Name', validators=[DataRequired()]) description = TextAreaField('Description', validators=[DataRequired()]) price = DecimalField('Price', validators=[DataRequired()]) category_id = IntegerField('Category ID', validators=[DataRequired()]) image = FileField('Product Image') submit = SubmitField('Create Product'). This defines a ProductForm with fields for the product's name (using StringField), description (using TextAreaField for longer text), price (using DecimalField for decimal values), category ID (using IntegerField), and image (using FileField for file uploads). The validators argument specifies validation rules. DataRequired() ensures that the field is not empty. A frequent question is: "What other field types are available?" Flask-WTF provides a wide range of field types, including FloatField, BooleanField, DateField, SelectField (for dropdown menus), and more. You can choose the appropriate field type based on the data you're collecting. Another common question: "How do I handle relationships in forms?" For foreign key relationships, like the category_id in our example, you might use a SelectField populated with the available categories from your database. You would query the database for the categories and then populate the choices attribute of the SelectField.

After defining the form class, you'll need to create an instance of it in your Flask view function: form = ProductForm(). Then, in your HTML template, you can render the form fields using Jinja2 templating: {{ form.name.label }} {{ form.name }} {{ form.description.label }} {{ form.description }} {{ form.price.label }} {{ form.price }} {{ form.category_id.label }} {{ form.category_id }} {{ form.image.label }} {{ form.image }} {{ form.submit }}. This renders the labels and input fields for each field in your form. A common practice is to wrap the form in a <form> tag and include the CSRF token for security: <form

method="POST"> {{ form.csrf_token }} ... </form>. The {{ form.csrf_token }} is crucial for protecting against Cross-Site Request Forgery attacks (OWASP, 2021). A frequent challenge is styling the form. You can use CSS to style the form elements to match your application's design. Bootstrap, a popular CSS framework, provides pre-styled form elements that you can easily integrate into your Flask templates. By using Flask-WTF and carefully designing your form, you create a user-friendly interface for adding new products to your catalog, while also ensuring that the data is validated and secure.

3.2 Handling form submissions in your Flask view.

Handling form submissions in a Flask view is the crucial next step after designing your "Create" form. Imagine you're building a platform for users to submit bug reports for a software project. You've designed a form with fields for the bug's title, description, severity, and the affected component. Now, you need to write the Flask view function that processes the form submission, validates the data, and stores it in the database. For Computer Engineering students and educators, understanding how to handle form submissions securely and efficiently is paramount. The process begins after you've defined your form class using Flask-WTF (or plain HTML) and created an instance of it in your Flask view function. The key is to check if the form has been submitted and if the submitted data is valid.

Within your Flask view function, you'll typically use an if statement to check if the request method is POST and if the form has been submitted: if request.method == 'POST' and form.validate_on_submit():. The form.validate_on_submit() method not only checks if the form has been submitted but also runs the validation rules you defined in your form class (e.g., DataRequired(), Email(), etc.). A frequent question is: "What happens if the form is not valid?" If the form is not valid, form.validate_on_submit() returns False, and you can re-render the form, displaying the validation errors to the user. Flask-WTF automatically makes these errors available to your template. You can access them using form.fieldname.errors, where fieldname is the name of the field. For example: {% for error in form.title.errors %} <div class="alert alert-danger">{{ error }}</div> {% endfor %}. This displays any errors associated with the title field. This allows the user to correct the invalid data before resubmitting the form.

If the form is valid, you can access the submitted data through the form object: title = form.title.data, description = form.description.data, severity = form.severity.data, component = form.component.data. This retrieves the data from the corresponding form fields. A common question is: "How do I handle file uploads?" For file uploads (using FileField), you can access the uploaded file using form.fieldname.data. This gives you a file object that you can then save to your server's file system or cloud storage. Remember to handle file uploads securely and validate the file type and size to prevent vulnerabilities. After retrieving the data, you can create a new record in your database using your SQLAlchemy models: new_bug_report = BugReport(title=title, description=description, severity=severity, component=component). Then, add the new record to the database session and commit the changes: db.session.add(new_bug_report); db.session.commit(). A frequent challenge is handling potential database errors. It's crucial to wrap your database operations in a try...except block to catch any exceptions that might occur, such as database connection errors or integrity errors. This prevents your application from crashing and allows you to display a user-friendly error message. Finally, after successfully creating the bug report, you can redirect the user to a success page or display a success message: return redirect(url_for('bug_reports')) or flash('Bug report submitted successfully!', 'success'). By carefully handling form submissions, validating data, and securely interacting with your database, you can create a robust and user-friendly "Create" functionality for your web application.

3.3 Implementing the "Create" logic: Inserting new records into the PostgreSQL database using your models.

Implementing the "Create" logic involves translating the data submitted through a form into new records within your PostgreSQL database. Consider an online learning platform where instructors can create new courses. The form collects information like the course title, description, instructor ID, and enrollment capacity. The "Create" logic takes this validated form data and persists it in the database. For Computer Engineering students and educators, understanding how to interact with the database using ORMs like SQLAlchemy is crucial for building data-driven applications. This process assumes you have already defined your database models using SQLAlchemy and handled the form submission in your Flask view, as discussed in previous sections. The key now is to use these models to create new records.

After validating the form data, you'll create an instance of your SQLAlchemy model, populating it with the data from the form. For example, if your course model is named Course, you'd do something like this: new_course = Course(title=form.title.data, description=form.description.data, instructor_id=form.instructor_id.data, capacity=form.capacity.data). This creates a new Course object in memory, but it's not yet saved to the database. A frequent question arises: "What if my model has relationships with other models?" If your Course model has a foreign key relationship with an Instructor model, for instance, and you're using a SelectField in your form to choose the instructor, the form.instructor_id.data will contain the ID of the selected instructor. SQLAlchemy will automatically handle the relationship when you commit the changes. However, for more complex relationships (like many-to-many), you might need to associate the related objects explicitly. For example, if a course can have multiple tags, you would need to fetch the tag objects from the database based on the selected tag IDs from the form and then add them to the tags attribute of the new_course object.

Once you've populated the model instance, you need to add it to the database session: db.session.add(new_course). This tells SQLAlchemy to prepare the new record for insertion into the database. A common question is: "What is a database session?" A database session is a temporary connection to the database that allows you to perform multiple operations (like adding, updating, or deleting records) as a single unit of work. This is important for maintaining data consistency. After adding the record to the session, you need to commit the changes to the database: db.session.commit(). This actually executes the SQL INSERT statement and persists the new record in the PostgreSQL database. A frequent challenge is handling potential database errors. It's crucial to wrap your database operations in a try...except block to catch any exceptions that might occur, such as database connection errors, integrity errors (e.g., trying to insert a record with a duplicate primary key), or other database-related issues. For example: try: db.session.add(new_course); db.session.commit() except IntegrityError as e: db.session.rollback(); print(f"Error creating course: {e}") return "Error creating course", 500. The db.session.rollback() part is essential. If an error occurs during the commit, you need to rollback the session to prevent partial updates to the database. By implementing the "Create" logic using SQLAlchemy models and proper error handling, you ensure that new records are inserted into your PostgreSQL database correctly and safely. This forms the backbone of the "Create" functionality in your web application.

3.4 Displaying success/error messages to the user after the create operation.

Providing feedback to the user after a "Create" operation is essential for a good user experience. Imagine a user submitting a complex form to register for a conference. They need to know if the registration was successful or if there were any issues, such as missing required fields or conflicts with existing registrations. Clear and informative messages guide the user and prevent confusion. For Computer Engineering students and educators, understanding how to provide effective feedback is crucial for building user-friendly applications. We'll explore how to display success and error messages in a Flask application after a create operation. The process assumes you've already handled the form submission and database interaction, as discussed in previous sections. The key now is to communicate the outcome to the user.

Flask provides a built-in mechanism for displaying messages called "flashing." These messages are stored in the session and can be accessed in your templates. To flash a message, you use the flash() function: flash('Course created successfully!', 'success') or flash('Error creating course. Please check the form.', 'danger'). The first argument is the message itself, and the second argument is the category of the message. Common categories include 'success', 'info', 'warning', and 'danger', which correspond to different visual styles (often used with Bootstrap). A frequent question is: "Where do I call the flash() function?" You typically call it after the database operation is complete, either successfully or with an error. If the course creation is successful, you flash a success message. If there's an error, you flash an error message. It's crucial to flash the message before redirecting the user, as the flashed messages are stored in the session, which might be cleared during redirection.

In your HTML template, you can then display the flashed messages. A common approach is to use a loop to iterate through the flashed messages and display them in alert boxes (using Bootstrap classes, for example): {% with messages = get_flashed_messages(with_categories=true) %} {% if messages %} {% for category, message in messages %} <div class="alert alert-{{ category }}">{{ message }}</div> {% endfor %} {% endif %} {% endwith %}. The get_flashed_messages(with_categories=true) function retrieves the flashed messages along with their categories. The loop iterates through the messages and displays them in alert boxes with the appropriate styling based on the category. A common question is: "How do I style the flashed messages?" You can use CSS to style the alert boxes to match your application's design. Bootstrap provides pre-styled alert classes that you can use directly. Another frequent question is: "How can I display more specific error messages?" Instead of generic error messages, you can provide more detailed information about the error. For example, if a database integrity error occurs (like a duplicate entry), you can flash a message that specifically mentions the duplicate field. This helps the user understand the issue and correct it. You can also pass variables to the flash() function using string formatting. By providing clear and informative success and error messages, you improve the user experience and make your application more user-friendly. This is a crucial aspect of building well-designed web applications.

3.5 Example: Creating a new product in the product catalog, a new blog post, or a new to-do item.

Let's walk through a concrete example of creating a new product in an e-commerce product catalog, tying together the concepts discussed in the previous sections. Imagine you're building an online store, and administrators need a way to add new products to the catalog. This involves a form for product details, handling the form submission, inserting the data into the database, and providing feedback to the administrator. For Computer Engineering students and educators, this example provides a practical application of the "Create" functionality in a web application. We'll use Flask, Flask-WTF for form handling, SQLAlchemy for database interaction, and Bootstrap for styling. Assume you've already set up your Flask project, PostgreSQL database, and defined your Product model using SQLAlchemy. You also have the necessary libraries installed.

First, create your Flask-WTF form class. Let's call it ProductForm: from flask_wtf import FlaskForm; from wtforms import StringField, TextAreaField, DecimalField, IntegerField, FileField, SubmitField; from wtforms.validators import DataRequired; class ProductForm(FlaskForm): name = StringField('Product Name', validators=[DataRequired()]) description = TextAreaField('Description', validators=[DataRequired()]) price = DecimalField('Price', validators=[DataRequired()]) category_id = IntegerField('Category ID', validators=[DataRequired()]) image = FileField('Product Image') submit = SubmitField('Create Product'). This form includes fields for the product's name, description, price, category ID, and image. Next, create your Flask view function to handle the form submission: @app.route('/products/create', methods=['GET', 'POST']) def create_product(): form = ProductForm() if request.method == 'POST' and form.validate_on_submit(): name = form.name.data description = form.description.data price = form.price.data category_id = form.category_id.data image = form.image.data # Handle image upload (save to file system or cloud storage) new_product = Product(name=name, description=description, price=price, category_id=category_id, image_url=image_url) # Replace image_url with the actual path db.session.add(new_product) try: db.session.commit() flash('Product created successfully!', 'success') return redirect(url_for('product_list')) # Redirect to product list page except Exception as e: db.session.rollback() flash(f'Error creating product: {e}', 'danger') return render_template('create_product.html', form=form) return render_template('create_product.html', form=form). This view function handles both GET (display the form) and POST (process the form submission) requests. It validates the form data, creates a new Product object, adds it to the database session, and commits the changes. It also includes error handling and flashes success or error messages.

Now, create your HTML template (create_product.html): {% extends "base.html" %} {% block content %} <h1>Create New Product</h1> <form method="POST" enctype="multipart/form-data"> {{ form.csrf_token }} {{ form.name.label }} {{ form.name }} {% for error in form.name.errors %} <div class="alert alert-danger">{{ error }}</div> {% endfor %} ... (similar for other fields) ... {{ form.submit }} </form> {% with messages = get_flashed_messages(with_categories=true) %} {% if messages %} {% for category, message in messages %} <div class="alert alert-{{ category }}">{{ message }}</div> {% endfor %} {% endif %} {% endwith %} {% endblock %}. This template renders the form fields, displays any validation errors, and shows flashed messages. Remember to handle the image upload appropriately. You'll need to save the uploaded file to your server's file system or a cloud storage service and store the file path or URL in the image_url field of your Product model. A common question is: "How do I handle image uploads securely?" Validate the file type and size to prevent malicious uploads. Consider using a dedicated storage service for production applications. By combining these steps, you create a functional "Create" feature for your product catalog, allowing administrators to add new products with ease. This example can be adapted for creating other types of data in your web application, such as blog posts or to-do items.

Chapter 4

Reading (R)

4.1 Retrieving data from the PostgreSQL database using your models.

Retrieving data from a PostgreSQL database using your models is a core operation in any data-driven web application. Imagine you're building an online library catalog. You need to display a list of books, search for books by title or author, and view details for a specific book. These actions all involve retrieving data from the database. For Computer Engineering students and educators, understanding how to efficiently and securely retrieve data using ORMs like SQLAlchemy is crucial. This discussion assumes you've already defined your database models using SQLAlchemy and established a connection to your PostgreSQL database, as covered in previous chapters. The key now is to use these models to query and retrieve the data you need.

SQLAlchemy provides a powerful query API for interacting with your database. Let's say you have a Book model with attributes like title, author, isbn, and publication_date. To retrieve all books, you can use the following query: books = Book.query.all(). This will return a list of all Book objects in your database. A frequent question arises: "What if I have a large number of books? Fetching all of them at once might be inefficient." For large datasets, you should use pagination. SQLAlchemy's query object provides methods like limit() and offset() to implement pagination. You can also use Flask-SQLAlchemy's Pagination object to simplify pagination. For example: page = request.args.get('page', 1, type=int); books = Book.query.paginate(page=page, per_page=10). This retrieves 10 books per page, and you can access the books for the current page using books.items. You can also use books.has_next and books.has_prev to determine if there are more pages.

To filter books based on certain criteria, you can use the filter() method. For example, to find books by a specific author: books = Book.query.filter(Book.author == 'Jane Austen').all(). You can also use more complex filter conditions: books = Book.query.filter(Book.title.like('%Pride%')).all(). This will find books whose titles contain the word "Pride." The like() operator allows for pattern matching using wildcards. A common question is: "How do I handle relationships when retrieving data?" If your Book model has a relationship with an Author model, you can access the author's information directly through the book object: for book in books: print(book.author.name). SQLAlchemy handles the join operations behind the scenes. You can also use the join() method to explicitly specify joins: books = Book.query.join(Author).filter(Author.name == 'Jane Austen').all(). This can be useful for optimizing queries. Another frequent question is: "How do I order the results?" You can use the order_by() method: books = Book.query.order_by(Book.publication_date.desc()).all(). This will order the books by publication date in descending order (newest first). By using SQLAlchemy's query API, you can efficiently and flexibly retrieve data from your PostgreSQL database, supporting various use cases in your web application. Remember to handle potential database errors using try...except blocks to ensure your application remains stable.

4.2 Displaying data on HTML pages using Jinja2 templating.

Displaying retrieved data on HTML pages is the crucial final step in the "Read" operation of CRUD. Imagine you've built a web application for an online store. You've retrieved a list of products from your PostgreSQL database using SQLAlchemy, as discussed previously. Now, you need to present this data to the user in a clear and organized way on your web pages. This is where Jinja2, a powerful templating engine for Python, comes into play. For Computer Engineering students and educators, understanding how to use templating engines like Jinja2 is essential for creating dynamic and maintainable web applications. Jinja2 allows you to embed Python code within your HTML templates, making it easy to dynamically generate content. The process begins after you've retrieved the data from your database in your Flask view function. You'll then pass this data to your HTML template.

Let's say you have a list of Product objects called products that you've retrieved from the database. In your Flask view function, you would render the template and pass the products list as a variable: return render_template('product_list.html', products=products). This makes the products variable available within your product_list.html template. Within your HTML template, you can use Jinja2's templating syntax to access and display the data. To loop through the products list, you would use a for loop: {% for product in products %} <h2>{{ product.name }}</h2> <p>{{ product.description }}</p> <p>Price: ${{

product.price }}</p> {% endfor %}. This loop iterates through each product object in the products list and displays its name, description, and price. A frequent question is: "How do I display data conditionally?" You can use if statements within your Jinja2 templates to control which parts of the template are rendered based on certain conditions. For example: {% if product.is_featured %} <span class="featured">Featured Product</span> {% endif %}. This will only display the "Featured Product" label if the is_featured attribute of the product is True.

Another common question is: "How do I handle more complex data structures, like nested objects or lists?" Jinja2 can handle these structures easily. You can access nested attributes using dot notation (e.g., product.category.name to access the name of the product's category). You can also use nested loops to iterate through lists of lists or other nested data structures. A frequent challenge is formatting data appropriately. Jinja2 provides filters that allow you to format data. For example, to format a date, you can use the strftime filter: {{ product.created_at | strftime('%Y-%m-%d') }}. You can also create custom filters to handle specific formatting needs. Remember that Jinja2 operates on the server-side. The HTML that is ultimately sent to the client's browser is just plain HTML. Jinja2 generates this HTML dynamically based on the data you pass to the template. This is what makes Jinja2 so powerful. By combining Jinja2's templating capabilities with the data retrieved from your PostgreSQL database, you can create dynamic and interactive web pages that display information in a user-friendly and visually appealing way. This dynamic data presentation is a cornerstone of modern web applications.

4.3 Implementing pagination for large datasets (if applicable).

Implementing pagination for large datasets is a crucial aspect of building scalable and user-friendly web applications. Imagine you're developing an e-commerce platform with thousands of products. Displaying all these products on a single page would be overwhelming for the user and would likely lead to performance issues. Pagination breaks down the large dataset into smaller, manageable pages, improving the user experience and reducing server load. For Computer Engineering students and educators, understanding pagination is essential for designing efficient and responsive web applications. The process typically involves retrieving data in chunks and providing navigation controls to move between pages. Let's explore how to implement pagination in a Flask application using SQLAlchemy and Jinja2. We'll assume you've already retrieved data from your PostgreSQL database using your models, as discussed in previous sections.

SQLAlchemy's query object provides methods like limit() and offset() that are fundamental to pagination. limit() specifies the maximum number of results to retrieve, and offset() specifies the starting point for the retrieval. However, manually calculating offsets can be cumbersome. Flask-SQLAlchemy's Pagination object simplifies this process. First, you need to determine the current page number. This is usually passed as a query parameter in the URL. You can retrieve it using page = request.args.get('page', 1, type=int). This retrieves the 'page' query parameter, defaulting to 1 if it's not present. The type=int ensures that the value is treated as an integer. Next, you can use the paginate() method on your SQLAlchemy query object: products =

Product.query.paginate(page=page, per_page=10). This retrieves 10 products for the specified page. The paginate() method returns a Pagination object, which provides helpful attributes like items (the list of products for the current page), has_next and has_prev (boolean values indicating if there are more pages), next_num and prev_num (the page numbers for the next and previous pages), and total (the total number of products).

In your Jinja2 template, you can then display the products for the current page: {% for product in products.items %} <h2>{{ product.name }}</h2> <p>{{ product.description }}</p> {% endfor %}. To create the pagination navigation controls, you can use Jinja2's conditional statements and loops: {% if products.has_prev %} <a href="{{ url_for('product_list', page=products.prev_num) }}">« Previous</a> {% endif %} {% for page in products.iter_pages() %} <a href="{{ url_for('product_list', page=page) }}" {% if products.page == page %}class="active"{% endif %}>{{ page }}</a> {% endfor %} {% if products.has_next %} <a href="{{ url_for('product_list', page=products.next_num) }}">Next »</a> {% endif %}. This creates "Previous" and "Next" links, as well as links for each page number. The products.iter_pages() method generates a list of page numbers to display, handling edge cases like not displaying too many page numbers. A common question is: "How do I style the pagination controls?" You can use CSS to style the links and make them more visually appealing. Bootstrap provides pre-styled pagination components that you can easily integrate into your templates. Another frequent question is: "How do I handle search or filter conditions along with pagination?" You'll need to include the search or filter parameters in the URL for the pagination links so that the correct data is retrieved for each page. By implementing pagination, you improve the performance and usability of your web application, making it easier for users to navigate through large datasets. This is a crucial consideration for any web application dealing with significant amounts of data.

4.4 Implementing search functionality (if applicable).

Implementing search functionality is a vital feature for many web applications, allowing users to quickly find the information they need within a larger dataset. Imagine building a platform for research papers. Users need to be able to search for papers by title, author, keywords, or abstract. For Computer Engineering students and educators, understanding how to implement efficient and effective search is crucial for building practical and user-friendly applications. The process typically involves creating a search form, handling the search query in your Flask view, querying the database based on the search terms, and displaying the results. Let's explore how to implement search functionality in a Flask application using SQLAlchemy and Jinja2. We'll assume you've already retrieved data from your PostgreSQL database using your models.

First, you need a search form in your HTML template. A simple form with a text input field and a submit button will suffice: <form method="GET"> <input type="text" name="search_query" placeholder="Search..."> <button type="submit">Search</button> </form>. The method="GET" attribute is important because we'll be passing the search query as a query parameter in the URL. The name="search_query" attribute is used to identify the search query in the request. In your Flask view function, you can retrieve the search query using search_query = request.args.get('search_query'). This retrieves the value of the search_query query parameter. A frequent question is: "What if the search query is empty?" You should handle this case gracefully. You can either display all results if the search query is empty or display a message indicating that no search term was provided.

Next, you need to query the database based on the search query. SQLAlchemy provides several ways to do this. A common approach is to use the like() operator for case-insensitive searches: results = Paper.query.filter(Paper.title.ilike(f'%{search_query}%')).all(). This will search for papers whose titles contain the search query, regardless of case. The ilike() operator performs a case-insensitive search. The f'%{search_query}%' syntax uses f-strings to create the search pattern with wildcards (%) at the beginning and end, allowing for partial matches. A common question is: "How do I search across multiple fields?" You can use the or_() operator to combine multiple filter conditions: from sqlalchemy import or_; results = Paper.query.filter(or_(Paper.title.ilike(f'%{search_query}%'), Paper.author.ilike(f'%{search_query}%'), Paper.keywords.ilike(f'%{search_query}%'))).all(). This will search for papers whose title, author, or keywords contain the search query. Another frequent question is: "How do I handle special characters in the search query?" You should sanitize the search query to prevent SQL injection vulnerabilities. SQLAlchemy's query API generally handles this automatically, but it's always good practice to be aware of potential security risks.

Finally, you need to display the search results in your HTML template. You can use Jinja2's templating features to loop through the results and display the relevant information: {% for paper in results %} <h2>{{ paper.title }}</h2> <p>Author: {{ paper.author }}</p> {% endfor %}. A common challenge is implementing pagination for search results. You can use the same pagination techniques discussed earlier, but remember to include the search query in the URL for the pagination links so that the correct results are displayed on each page. By implementing search functionality, you make it easier for users to find the information they need within your web application. This is a crucial aspect of building user-friendly and effective applications.

4.5 Example: Displaying a list of products, blog posts, or to-do items. Displaying details of a single item.

Let's illustrate the "Read" functionality with a concrete example: displaying a list of products in an e-commerce catalog and then viewing the details of a single product. Imagine you're building an online store. Users should be able to browse a list of available products and then click on a product to see its detailed description, price, and images. For Computer Engineering students and educators, this example demonstrates a practical application of retrieving and displaying data in a web application. We'll use Flask, SQLAlchemy, and Jinja2 to implement this functionality. Assume you've already set up your Flask project, PostgreSQL database, and defined your Product model using SQLAlchemy.

First, let's create the Flask view function to display the list of products: @app.route('/products') def product_list(): products = Product.query.all() return render_template('product_list.html', products=products).1 This view function retrieves all products from the database using Product.query.all() and passes them to the product_list.html template. Next, create the product_list.html template: {% extends "base.html" %} {% block content %} <h1>Product Catalog</h1> <ul> {% for product in products %} <li><a href="{{ url_for('product_details', product_id=product.id) }}">{{ product.name }}</a></li> {% endfor %} </ul> {% endblock %}. This template displays a list of product names, each linked to the product details page. The url_for('product_details', product_id=product.id) generates the URL for the product details page, passing the product ID as a parameter. A common question is: "How do I handle a large number of products?" You should implement pagination, as discussed in the previous section, to avoid displaying all products on a single page.

Now, let's create the Flask view function to display the details of a single product: @app.route('/products/<int:product_id>') def product_details(product_id): product = Product.query.get_or_404(product_id) return render_template('product_details.html', product=product).2 This view function retrieves the product with the specified ID using Product.query.get_or_404(product_id). The get_or_404() method is a convenient way to handle cases where the product is not found. It automatically returns a 404 error if the product doesn't exist. Next, create the product_details.html template: {% extends "base.html" %} {% block content %} <h1>{{ product.name }}</h1> <p>{{ product.description }}</p> <p>Price: ${{ product.price }}</p> <img src="{{ product.image_url }}" alt="{{ product.name }}"> {% endblock %}. This template displays the details of the selected product, including its name, description, price, and image. A frequent question is:

"How do I handle related data, like the product's category or manufacturer?" If your Product model has relationships with other models (e.g., Category, Manufacturer), you can access the related data directly in your template: {{ product.category.name }}. SQLAlchemy will handle the necessary database joins.

A common challenge is handling cases where the product image is missing. You can use Jinja2's conditional statements to display a placeholder image if the image_url is null: {% if product.image_url %} <img src="{{ product.image_url }}" alt="{{ product.name }}"> {% else %} <img src="placeholder.jpg" alt="No Image Available"> {% endif %}. Another frequent question is: "How do I style the product details page?" You can use CSS to style the page and make it more visually appealing. Bootstrap provides pre-styled components that you can easily integrate into your templates. By combining these steps, you create a user-friendly way to browse and view product details in your online store. This example can be adapted for displaying other types of data in your web application, such as blog posts or to-do items. Remember to handle potential errors, such as database connection errors or cases where a product is not found, to ensure a robust and user-friendly experience.

Chapter 5

Updating (U)

5.1 Designing the "Update" form (often similar to the "Create" form, but pre-filled with existing data).

Designing an "Update" form is a crucial part of implementing the update functionality in a web application. Imagine you're building a content management system (CMS) for a blog. Authors need to be able to edit their existing blog posts, correcting typos, updating information, or adding new content. The "Update" form provides the interface for making these changes. For Computer Engineering students and educators, understanding how to create and pre-populate update forms is essential for building dynamic and user-friendly applications. Often, the "Update" form is very similar to the "Create" form, but with one key difference: it's pre-filled with the existing data for the item being updated. This allows the user to see the current values and easily modify them. Let's walk through the process using Flask-WTF.

The first step is often to reuse your existing "Create" form class. Since the structure and fields are likely the same, you can inherit from it or directly use it. If there are fields you don't want editable in the update form, you can either omit them in the template or set them as disabled. For example, if the created_at timestamp shouldn't be changed, you can simply not include it in the form rendering in your template. A frequent question is: "What if I need to add or remove fields in the update form?"

If there are fields specific only to the update process, you can add them to the form class. If you need a completely different form structure, you can create a separate form class. For most common cases, reusing or slightly modifying the "Create" form is the most efficient approach.

The crucial difference with the "Update" form is that it needs to be populated with the existing data. In your Flask view function, after retrieving the object you want to update from the database (e.g., post = Post.query.get_or_404(post_id)), you need to populate the form with this data. You can do this when you instantiate the form: form = PostForm(obj=post). The obj argument takes the object whose data you want to pre-fill the form with. This will automatically populate the form fields with the corresponding attributes of the post object. A common question is: "What if my form has fields that are not directly mapped to the object's attributes?" You can manually set the values of individual fields after instantiating the form. For example, if you have a category_name field in the form but the Post model only has a category_id, you can query the category name separately and then set the value of the form field: form.category_name.data = post.category.name.

In your HTML template, you render the form just like you would with the "Create" form: {{ form.title.label }} {{ form.title }} .... Because the form is pre-populated, the user will see the existing values in the input fields. A frequent challenge is handling relationships in the update form. If you have a foreign key relationship, you'll likely use a SelectField to allow the user to choose a related object. You'll need to populate the choices for the SelectField with the available related objects from the database. You can do this in your view function before instantiating the form. For many-to-many relationships, you might use a series of checkboxes or a more complex UI element. The key is to ensure that the form reflects the current state of the related objects. By pre-filling the "Update" form with existing data, you provide a user-friendly interface that makes it easy for users to modify their data accurately and efficiently. This is a fundamental part of the "Update" functionality in any web application.

5.2 Retrieving the record to be updated from the database.

Retrieving the correct record to be updated from the database is a critical step in the "Update" process. Imagine you're building a project management application. A project manager needs to edit the details of a specific task, such as its description, due date, or assigned team members. Before the update form can be displayed, the application must retrieve the correct task from the database based on its unique identifier. For Computer Engineering students and educators, understanding how to efficiently and securely retrieve records for updates is essential for building robust and reliable applications. This process assumes you have already defined your database models using SQLAlchemy and have a way to identify the record to be updated, typically through a unique identifier like a primary key.

The most common approach is to use the get() or get_or_404() methods provided by SQLAlchemy. Let's say your Task model has an id field as its primary key. To retrieve a task with a specific ID, you would use: task = Task.query.get(task_id). The get() method takes the primary key value as an argument and returns the corresponding record if found, or None if not. A frequent question is: "What happens if the record is not found?" You should handle this case gracefully. You can either display an error message to the user or redirect them to a different page. The get_or_404() method provides a convenient way to handle this scenario. If the record is not found, it automatically raises a 404 error, which can be handled by your Flask application. Using task = Task.query.get_or_404(task_id) simplifies the process and makes your code more concise.

Another common approach, especially when dealing with more complex queries or when you need to apply additional filters, is to use the filter() method in conjunction with first() or one_or_404(). For example, if you want to retrieve a task by its name and project ID, you would use: task = Task.query.filter(Task.name == task_name, Task.project_id == project_id).first(). The first() method returns the first matching record or None if no record is found. Similarly, one_or_404() works like get_or_404(), but for queries with filters instead of just the primary key. A frequent question is: "When should I use get() vs. filter()?" Use get() when you are retrieving a record based on its primary key. It's the most efficient way to do so. Use filter() when you need to apply additional filters or when you are not retrieving by primary key.

A crucial aspect of retrieving records for updates is security. Ensure that the user has the necessary authorization to update the record. For example, in our project management application, you might want to ensure that only the project manager or a team member assigned to the task can update it. You can implement authorization checks in your view function before retrieving the record. This prevents unauthorized users from modifying data they shouldn't have access to. After retrieving the correct record, you can then pre-populate the update form with the data from this record, as discussed in the previous section. This allows the user to see the current values and easily make changes. By following these best practices, you can ensure that you are retrieving the correct record for updates securely and efficiently, laying the foundation for a smooth and reliable update process.

5.3 Handling form submissions for updates.

Handling form submissions for updates is a critical part of the update functionality in a web application. Imagine a user editing their profile information on a social media platform. They've made changes to their bio, profile picture, and contact details. The application needs to process this submitted form data, validate it, and then update the corresponding user record in the database. For Computer Engineering students and educators, understanding how to handle form submissions for updates securely and efficiently is crucial for building robust and user-friendly applications. This process assumes you have already retrieved the record to be updated from the database and pre-populated the update form, as discussed in the previous sections. The key now is to process the submitted form data.

Within your Flask view function, you'll typically use an if statement to check if the request method is POST and if the form has been submitted and validated: if request.method == 'POST' and form.validate_on_submit():. The form.validate_on_submit() method, as discussed before, handles both the submission check and the validation rules you defined in your form class. A frequent question is: "What happens if the form is not valid?" If the form is not valid, form.validate_on_submit() returns False. You should re-render the form, displaying the validation errors to the user. Flask-WTF automatically makes these errors available to your template, which you can then display next to the corresponding fields. This allows the user to correct the invalid data before resubmitting.

If the form is valid, you can access the submitted data through the form object: bio = form.bio.data, profile_picture = form.profile_picture.data, contact_details = form.contact_details.data. This retrieves the data from the corresponding form fields. A common question is: "How do I handle file uploads for updates?" File uploads for updates are handled similarly to file uploads for creation. You access the uploaded file using form.fieldname.data and then save it to your server's file system or cloud storage. However, you might also want to provide the user with the option to not change the existing file. In this case, you would check if a new file was uploaded. If not, you would keep the existing file path in your database. After retrieving the data, you then update the existing record in your database. Since you've already retrieved the record from the database, you can directly modify its attributes: user.bio = bio, user.profile_picture = profile_picture, user.contact_details = contact_details. Then, commit the changes to the database: db.session.commit(). A frequent challenge is handling potential database errors. It's crucial to wrap your database operations in a try...except block to catch any exceptions that might occur, such as database connection errors or integrity errors (e.g., trying to update a record with a duplicate unique key).

Finally, after successfully updating the record, you should provide feedback to the user. You can use Flask's flashing mechanism to display a success message: flash('Profile updated successfully!', 'success'). Then, redirect the user to a different page or refresh the current page. A best practice is to redirect after a successful update to prevent accidental resubmissions if the user refreshes the page. By carefully handling form submissions for updates, validating data, and securely interacting with your database, you can create a smooth and reliable update process for your web application. This is a fundamental part of managing data effectively in any web application.

5.4 Implementing the "Update" logic: Modifying existing records in the PostgreSQL database.

Implementing the "Update" logic involves translating the validated form data into modifications of existing records within your PostgreSQL database. Imagine a scenario where you're building a learning management system (LMS). Instructors need to be able to update course details, such as the course description, syllabus, or assigned readings. The "Update" logic takes the validated form data and applies these changes to the corresponding course record in the database. For Computer Engineering students and educators, understanding how to interact with the database using ORMs like SQLAlchemy to perform updates is crucial for building data-driven applications. This process assumes you've already retrieved the record to be updated from the database and handled the form submission, as discussed in previous sections. The key now is to use the retrieved model instance and the validated form data to modify the existing record.

After validating the form data, you'll have the existing model instance (e.g., course) that you retrieved from the database and the data from the submitted form (e.g., form.description.data, form.syllabus.data). You can now directly modify the attributes of the model instance with the new data: course.description = form.description.data, course.syllabus = form.syllabus.data. This updates the course object in memory, but it's not yet reflected in the database. A frequent question arises: "What if my model has relationships with other models?" If your Course model has a foreign key relationship with an Instructor model, and you're using a SelectField in your form to choose the instructor, the form data will contain the ID of the selected instructor. You would update the foreign key attribute of the course object: course.instructor_id = form.instructor_id.data. SQLAlchemy will handle the relationship update when you commit the changes. For many-to-many relationships, you'll likely need to manage the association table directly. This often involves adding or removing entries in the association table based on the submitted form data.

Once you've updated the model instance with the new data, you need to commit the changes to the database. This is done through the database session: db.session.commit(). This command executes the SQL UPDATE statement and persists the changes to the PostgreSQL database. A common question is: "Do I need to add the object to the session before committing?" No, you don't need to add the object to the session if you retrieved it from the session initially. The object is already attached to the session. You only need to add objects to the session when you are creating new records. A frequent challenge is handling potential database errors. It's crucial to wrap your database operations in a try...except block to catch any exceptions that might occur, such as database connection errors or integrity errors. For example: try: db.session.commit() except IntegrityError as e: db.session.rollback(); print(f"Error updating course: {e}") return "Error updating course",

500. The db.session.rollback() part is essential. If an error occurs during the commit, you need to rollback the session to prevent partial updates to the database. By implementing the "Update" logic using SQLAlchemy model instances and proper error handling, you ensure that existing records are modified correctly and safely in your PostgreSQL database. This forms the core of the "Update" functionality in your web application.

5.5 Displaying success/error messages.

Displaying appropriate success or error messages to the user after an update operation is crucial for a positive user experience. Imagine a user editing their profile on a social media platform. After submitting the updated information, they need to know if the changes were saved successfully or if there were any issues, such as invalid data or database errors. Clear and informative messages provide feedback and guide the user. For Computer Engineering students and educators, understanding how to provide effective feedback is essential for building user-friendly applications. This discussion assumes you've already handled the form submission and database interaction for the update operation. The key now is to communicate the outcome to the user in a meaningful way.

Flask's flashing mechanism, as discussed in the "Create" chapter, is also ideal for displaying messages after an update. You use the flash() function to store a message in the session, which can then be displayed in your templates. For example, flash('Profile updated successfully!', 'success') or flash('Error updating profile. Please check the form.', 'danger'). The first argument is the message itself, and the second is the category, which helps with styling (e.g., using Bootstrap alert classes). A frequent question is: "When should I call the flash() function?" Call it after the database operation is complete, whether successfully or with an error. It's crucial to flash the message before any redirection, as the flashed messages are stored in the session, which might be cleared during a redirect.

In your HTML template, you can display flashed messages using a loop and conditional logic: {% with messages = get_flashed_messages(with_categories=true) %} {% if messages %} {% for category, message in messages %} <div class="alert alert-{{ category }}">{{ message }}</div> {% endfor %} {% endif %} {% endwith %}. This code retrieves the flashed messages along with their categories and displays them in alert boxes. A common question is: "How do I style these messages?" You can use CSS to style the alert boxes. Bootstrap's alert classes (e.g., alert-success, alert-danger, alert-warning) are commonly used for this purpose. Another frequent question is: "How can I display more specific error messages?" Instead of generic error messages, provide context-specific information. For instance, if a database integrity error occurs (e.g., a duplicate username), flash a message like "Username already exists. Please choose a different one." This helps the user understand the exact problem. You can also use string formatting within the flash message to include details about the error.

A best practice is to log errors on the server-side, even if you display a user-friendly message. This helps with debugging and monitoring your application. Use Python's logging module for this purpose. For example: import logging; logging.error(f"Error updating profile: {e}"). This logs the error details to your server logs. By providing clear, specific, and styled success and error messages, you significantly improve the user experience. This is a fundamental aspect of building well-designed and user-friendly web applications. Remember to balance providing enough information to the user without revealing sensitive system details in error messages.

5.6 Example: Editing an existing product, blog post, or to-do item.

Let's illustrate the "Update" functionality with a practical example: editing an existing product in an e-commerce catalog. Imagine you're building an online store, and administrators need a way to modify product details, such as the name, description, price, or category. This involves retrieving the product data, pre-filling an update form, handling the form submission, updating the database, and providing feedback to the administrator. For Computer Engineering students and educators, this example demonstrates a real-world application of the "Update" functionality in a web application. We'll use Flask, Flask-WTF, SQLAlchemy, and Bootstrap. Assume you have your Flask project set up, PostgreSQL database configured, Product model defined, and necessary libraries installed.

First, create your Flask-WTF form (if you haven't already; you can often reuse your "Create" form): from flask_wtf import FlaskForm; from wtforms import StringField, TextAreaField, DecimalField, IntegerField, FileField, SubmitField; from wtforms.validators import DataRequired; class ProductForm(FlaskForm): name = StringField('Product Name', validators=[DataRequired()]) description = TextAreaField('Description', validators=[DataRequired()]) price = DecimalField('Price', validators=[DataRequired()]) category_id = IntegerField('Category ID', validators=[DataRequired()]) image = FileField('Product Image') submit = SubmitField('Update Product'). Next, create your Flask view function: @app.route('/products/edit/<int:product_id>', methods=['GET', 'POST']) def edit_product(product_id): product = Product.query.get_or_404(product_id) form = ProductForm(obj=product) # Pre-fill the form with product data if request.method == 'POST' and form.validate_on_submit(): product.name = form.name.data product.description = form.description.data product.price = form.price.data product.category_id = form.category_id.data if form.image.data: # Only update image if a new one is uploaded product.image_url = handle_image_upload(form.image.data) # Replace with your image upload function try: db.session.commit() flash('Product updated successfully!', 'success') return redirect(url_for('product_list')) except Exception as e: db.session.rollback() flash(f'Error updating product: {e}', 'danger') return render_template('edit_product.html', form=form, product=product) return render_template('edit_product.html', form=form, product=product). This view function retrieves the product, pre-fills the form, handles POST requests (updates), and includes error handling and flash messages.

Create your HTML template (edit_product.html): {% extends "base.html" %} {% block content %} <h1>Edit Product</h1> <form method="POST" enctype="multipart/form-data"> {{ form.csrf_token }} {{ form.name.label }} {{ form.name }} {% for error in form.name.errors %} <div class="alert alert-danger">{{ error }}</div> {% endfor %} ... (similar for other fields) ... {{ form.submit }} </form> {% with messages =

get_flashed_messages(with_categories=true) %} {% if messages %} {% for category, message in messages %} <div class="alert alert-{{ category }}">{{ message }}</div> {% endfor %} {% endif %} {% endwith %} {% endblock %}. This template renders the pre-filled form, displays errors, and shows flash messages. Remember to implement the handle_image_upload function for secure image handling. A crucial point is handling the image upload. You likely only want to update the image_url if a *new* image is uploaded. The example code reflects this logic. A common question is: "How do I handle related data?" Similar to creating, if you have related models, you'll need to update those relationships as well. For many-to-many relationships, this often involves managing the association table directly. By combining these steps, you create a functional "Edit" feature. This example can be adapted for editing other data types, like blog posts or to-do items. Always prioritize secure file handling and robust error management in your implementation.

Chapter 6

Deleting (D)

6.1 Implementing the "Delete" functionality: Adding a "Delete" button or link to your HTML pages.

Implementing the "Delete" functionality involves adding a way for users to initiate the deletion of a record from your database. Imagine you're building a task management application. Users should be able to delete tasks they no longer need. This requires adding a "Delete" button or link to the interface, triggering the deletion process. For Computer Engineering students and educators, understanding how to implement delete functionality securely and efficiently is essential for building robust and user-friendly applications. We'll explore how to add a "Delete" button or link to your HTML pages within a Flask application. The process assumes you've already retrieved the data you want to display (e.g., a list of tasks) and are displaying it in your HTML template.

The simplest approach is to add a button or link within your HTML template for each item that can be deleted. Let's say you're displaying a list of tasks. Within your Jinja2 template, inside the loop that iterates through the tasks, you would add the delete button or link: {% for task in tasks %} <li>{{ task.name }} <form method="POST" action="{{ url_for('delete_task', task_id=task.id) }}" style="display: inline;"> {{ form.csrf_token }} <button type="submit" onclick="return confirm('Are you sure you want to delete this task?')">Delete</button>

</form> </li> {% endfor %}. This adds a button next to each task. The action attribute of the form specifies the URL that will handle the delete operation. The url_for('delete_task', task_id=task.id) generates the URL, passing the task ID as a parameter. A crucial aspect is the onclick event handler. return confirm('Are you sure you want to delete this task?') displays a confirmation dialog to the user before the deletion is initiated. This helps prevent accidental deletions. A frequent question is: "Why use a POST request for delete?" Using a POST request for delete operations is a best practice for security. It prevents accidental deletions by simply visiting a URL. POST requests are typically used for actions that modify data on the server.

Another common approach is to use a link instead of a button: <a href="{{ url_for('delete_task', task_id=task.id) }}" onclick="return confirm('Are you sure you want to delete this task?')">Delete</a>. This works similarly to the button approach, but uses a link instead. A common question is: "How do I style the delete button or link?" You can use CSS to style the button or link to match your application's design. Bootstrap provides pre-styled button classes that you can easily integrate into your templates. A frequent challenge is handling CSRF protection for delete operations. Since we're using a POST request, we need to include the CSRF token in the form. This is done using {{ form.csrf_token }} within the form. This is essential for preventing Cross-Site Request Forgery (CSRF) attacks (OWASP, 2021). You will need to ensure you are passing the form to your template. You can simply pass an empty form if you are not using a form on the page. By adding a "Delete" button or link with a confirmation dialog and CSRF protection, you provide a user-friendly and secure way for users to initiate the deletion of records in your web application.

6.2 Handling delete requests in your Flask view.

Handling delete requests in your Flask view is the crucial next step after adding the "Delete" button or link to your HTML pages. Imagine a user clicking the "Delete" button next to a product in an online store. This action sends a request to your Flask application, which needs to process this request, verify the user's authorization, and then delete the product record from the database. For Computer Engineering students and educators, understanding how to handle delete requests securely and efficiently is paramount for building robust and reliable web applications. This discussion focuses on processing the delete request within your Flask view function. We assume you have added the "Delete" button or link to your HTML template, as discussed in the previous section.

The key is to create a Flask view function that corresponds to the URL you specified in the action attribute of your delete form or link. Let's say you named your view function delete_task and the URL is /tasks/delete/<int:task_id>. The <int:task_id> part of the URL captures the task ID, which is passed as an argument to the view function: @app.route('/tasks/delete/<int:task_id>', methods=['POST']) def delete_task(task_id):. Notice that the methods argument is set to POST. As discussed earlier, using POST for delete operations is a security best practice. Inside your view function, the first step is to retrieve the task to be deleted from the database: task = Task.query.get_or_404(task_id). The get_or_404() method is a convenient way to retrieve the task by ID and handle the case where the task is not found. It automatically raises a 404 error if the task doesn't exist. A frequent question is: "What if the user tries to delete a task that doesn't exist?" The get_or_404() method handles this gracefully, preventing your application from crashing.

The next crucial step is authorization. You need to ensure that the user has the necessary permissions to delete the task. This might involve checking if the user is the owner of the task or has administrative privileges. You can implement authorization checks using Flask's authentication and authorization mechanisms. If the user is not authorized, you should return a 403 Forbidden error: abort(403). A common question is: "How do I implement authorization?" Flask extensions like Flask-Login can help with user authentication, and you can define your own authorization logic based on user roles or permissions. After verifying the user's authorization, you can proceed with deleting the task: db.session.delete(task). This marks the task for deletion in the database session. A frequent challenge is handling potential database errors. It's crucial to wrap your database operations in a try...except block to catch any exceptions that might occur, such as database connection errors or integrity errors (e.g., if there are related records that prevent the deletion). For example: try: db.session.commit() except IntegrityError as e: db.session.rollback(); flash('Error deleting task. Please check for related records.', 'danger'); return redirect(url_for('task_list')). The db.session.rollback() part is essential. If an error occurs during the commit, you need to rollback the session to prevent partial updates to the database.

Finally, after successfully deleting the task, you should provide feedback to the user. You can use Flask's flashing mechanism to display a success message: flash('Task deleted successfully!', 'success'). Then, redirect the user to a different page, such as the task list page: return redirect(url_for('task_list')). By carefully handling delete requests, implementing authorization checks, and managing potential database errors, you can create a secure and reliable delete functionality for your web application. This is a crucial aspect of data management in any web application.

6.3 Implementing the "Delete" logic: Removing records from the PostgreSQL database.

Implementing the "Delete" logic involves translating the delete request into the actual removal of a record from your PostgreSQL database. Imagine a user deleting a comment on a blog post. The application needs to identify the correct comment record in the database and then permanently remove it. For Computer Engineering students and educators, understanding how to interact with the database to perform deletions efficiently and safely is essential for building robust and reliable web applications. This discussion assumes you have already handled the delete request in your Flask view function and verified the user's authorization to delete the record, as discussed in previous sections. The key now is to use the retrieved model instance to remove the corresponding record from the database.

After retrieving the model instance that represents the record to be deleted (e.g., comment = Comment.query.get_or_404(comment_id)), the actual deletion process is straightforward with SQLAlchemy. You use the db.session.delete() method, passing the model instance as an argument: db.session.delete(comment). This marks the comment object for deletion within the current database session. It's important to understand that this *doesn't* immediately delete the record from the database. The deletion is only performed when you commit the changes to the session. A frequent question is: "What happens if I try to delete a record that has related records in other tables?" If you have foreign key constraints defined in your database, PostgreSQL will prevent the deletion if there are related records. You'll need to handle this situation appropriately. You might need to delete the related records first or update the foreign key relationships to point to a different record. SQLAlchemy provides mechanisms for handling cascading deletes, which can automatically delete related records when a parent record is deleted. You can define these cascading options in your model definitions.

After marking the record for deletion, you need to commit the changes to the database: db.session.commit(). This executes the SQL DELETE statement and permanently removes the record from the PostgreSQL database. A common question is: "What is the database session, and why do I need it?" The database session is a temporary connection to the database that allows you to perform multiple operations (like adding, updating, or deleting records) as a single unit of work. This is crucial for maintaining data consistency. All operations within a session are treated as a transaction. If any error occurs during the transaction, you can rollback the session, undoing all changes made within that session. A frequent challenge is handling potential database errors. It's crucial to wrap your database operations in a try...except block to catch any exceptions that might occur, such as database connection errors, integrity errors (e.g., if a foreign key constraint prevents the deletion), or other database-related issues. For example: try:

db.session.delete(comment); db.session.commit() except IntegrityError as e: db.session.rollback(); flash('Error deleting comment. Please check for replies or related records.', 'danger'); return redirect(url_for('blog_post', post_id=comment.post_id)). The db.session.rollback() part is essential. If an error occurs during the commit, you need to rollback the session to prevent partial updates to the database. By implementing the delete logic using SQLAlchemy and proper error handling, you ensure that records are removed from your PostgreSQL database correctly and safely. This forms the core of the "Delete" functionality in your web application.

6.4 Confirmation dialogs before deleting (important for preventing accidental deletions).

Implementing confirmation dialogs before deleting records is a crucial step in preventing accidental data loss and ensuring a good user experience. Imagine a user browsing a list of their saved files. Accidentally clicking a "Delete" button without a confirmation could lead to the irreversible loss of important data. Confirmation dialogs act as a safety net, giving users a chance to double-check their decision before proceeding with the deletion. For Computer Engineering students and educators, understanding how to implement these dialogs effectively is crucial for building user-friendly and robust applications. This discussion focuses on implementing confirmation dialogs using JavaScript within your HTML templates.

The core idea is to use JavaScript's confirm() function, which displays a dialog box with an "OK" and "Cancel" button. This function returns true if the user clicks "OK" and false if they click "Cancel." You can use this return value to control whether the delete operation proceeds. The most common approach is to attach this confirmation dialog to the onclick event of your delete button or link. Let's say you have a delete button within a loop that displays a list of files: {% for file in files %} <li>{{ file.name }} <form method="POST" action="{{ url_for('delete_file', file_id=file.id) }}" style="display: inline;"> {{ form.csrf_token }} <button type="submit" onclick="return confirm('Are you sure you want to delete this file?')">Delete</button> </form> </li> {% endfor %}. The crucial part is the onclick event handler: onclick="return confirm('Are you sure you want to delete this file?')" This JavaScript code will be executed when the user clicks the "Delete" button. The confirm() function displays the confirmation dialog with the message "Are you sure you want to delete this file?". If the user clicks "OK," the function returns true, and the form submission proceeds, initiating the delete operation. If the user clicks "Cancel," the function returns false, and the form submission is cancelled, preventing the deletion.

A frequent question is: "Can I customize the message in the confirmation dialog?" Yes, you can change the text within the confirm() function to be more specific to the item being deleted. For example, you could include the file name: onclick="return confirm('Are you sure you want to delete {{ file.name }}?')" This would display a dialog like "Are you sure you want to delete my_document.pdf?". This provides more context to the user and further reduces the risk of accidental deletions. Another common question is: "How do I handle cases where the delete operation is initiated through a link instead of a button?" The approach is similar. You can attach the onclick event handler to the <a> tag: <a

href="{{ url_for('delete_file', file_id=file.id) }}" onclick="return confirm('Are you sure you want to delete this file?')">Delete</a>. The principle is the same; the confirmation dialog will be displayed before the link is followed. A frequent challenge is ensuring that the confirmation dialog is displayed for all delete operations, even if they are initiated through different parts of the interface. A good practice is to encapsulate the confirmation logic in a reusable JavaScript function that you can call from any delete button or link. By implementing confirmation dialogs, you add a crucial layer of protection against accidental data deletions, significantly improving the user experience and data integrity of your application. This is a fundamental aspect of building robust and user-friendly web applications.

6.5 Example: Deleting a product, blog post, or to-do item.

Let's illustrate the "Delete" functionality with a concrete example: deleting a product from an e-commerce catalog. Imagine you're managing an online store, and you need to remove a product that is no longer available or has been discontinued. This involves providing a way to initiate the deletion (e.g., a "Delete" button), handling the delete request, removing the product from the database, and providing feedback to the user. For Computer Engineering students and educators, this example demonstrates a practical application of the "Delete" functionality in a web application. We'll use Flask, SQLAlchemy, and Jinja2. Assume you've already set up your Flask project, PostgreSQL database, and defined your Product model using SQLAlchemy.

First, add a "Delete" button (or link) to your product list page. Within your product_list.html template, inside the loop that displays the products, add the following: {% for product in products %} <li>{{ product.name }} <form method="POST" action="{{ url_for('delete_product', product_id=product.id) }}" style="display: inline;"> {{ form.csrf_token }} <button type="submit" onclick="return confirm('Are you sure you want to delete {{ product.name }}?')">Delete</button> </form> </li> {% endfor %}. This adds a "Delete" button next to each product. The action attribute of the form points to the delete_product view function, passing the product ID. The onclick event handler displays a confirmation dialog before submitting the form. Remember to ensure that you are passing a form object to your template context, even if it is an empty form. This is necessary for the CSRF token to be included in the form. A frequent question is: "Why include the CSRF token?" The CSRF token protects against Cross-Site Request Forgery attacks. It ensures that the delete request originated from your website and not from a malicious third party.

Next, create the Flask view function to handle the delete request: @app.route('/products/delete/<int:product_id>', methods=['POST']) def delete_product(product_id): product = Product.query.get_or_404(product_id) if not current_user.is_admin: # Example authorization check; adapt to your needs abort(403) try: db.session.delete(product) db.session.commit() flash('Product deleted successfully!', 'success') except Exception as e: db.session.rollback() flash(f'Error deleting product: {e}', 'danger') return redirect(url_for('product_list')). This view function retrieves the product, checks for authorization (replace with your actual authorization logic), deletes the product from the database, handles potential errors, and flashes a success or error message. A common question is: "How do I implement authorization?" You'll need to integrate an authentication system (e.g., using Flask-Login) and define your authorization rules (e.g., based on user roles).

Finally, ensure that your template displays flashed messages: {% with messages = get_flashed_messages(with_categories=true) %} {% if messages %} {% for category, message in messages %} <div class="alert alert-{{ category }}">{{ message }}</div> {% endfor %} {% endif %} {% endwith %}. This displays the success or error messages to the user after the delete operation. A frequent challenge is handling related records. If your Product model has relationships with other models (e.g., OrderItems), you might need to handle those relationships before deleting a product. You could either delete the related records first or update the foreign key relationships. Consider using cascading deletes in your model definitions to automate this process. By combining these steps, you create a functional "Delete" feature for your product catalog. This example can be adapted for deleting other data types, like blog posts or to-do items. Always prioritize secure authorization checks and robust error management in your implementation.

Chapter 7

Enhancements and Best Practices

7.1 Input validation: Ensuring data integrity by validating user input on the server-side.

Input validation is a cornerstone of building secure and reliable web applications. Imagine a user filling out a registration form on a social media platform. Without proper validation, they could enter invalid data, such as a malformed email address, a password that's too short, or even malicious code disguised as input. Server-side input validation acts as the last line of defense, ensuring that only clean and valid data is processed by your application. For Computer Engineering students and educators, mastering input validation techniques is crucial for preventing vulnerabilities and maintaining data integrity. While client-side validation can enhance the user experience by providing immediate feedback, it should never be relied upon as the sole means of validation. Client-side validation can be easily bypassed by a determined attacker, making server-side validation absolutely essential.

The process begins after you've received the user input, typically through a form submission. In a Flask application, you'll often use Flask-WTF to handle form data and validation. You define validation rules within your form class using validators provided by WTForms. For example: username = StringField('Username', validators=[DataRequired(), Length(min=3, max=20)]). This defines a username field that is required (DataRequired()) and must be between 3 and 20 characters long (Length()). A frequent question is: "What other validators are available?" WTForms provides a wide range of validators, including Email, URL, EqualTo, NumberRange, and custom validators. You can choose the appropriate validators based on the type of data you're validating. A crucial aspect of input validation is handling validation errors gracefully. If validation fails, you should display informative error messages to the user, indicating which fields have invalid data and why. Flask-WTF makes these errors available to your template, allowing you to display them next to the corresponding form fields.

Beyond basic field validation, you often need to validate data in the context of your application's logic. For example, you might need to check if a username is already taken or if a given date is within a valid range. You can implement custom validation functions to handle these scenarios. These functions can access the database or other resources to perform more complex validation checks. A common question is: "How do I implement custom validators?" You can define custom validators as functions that take the form and the field as arguments and raise a ValidationError if the data is invalid. You can then add these custom validators to the validators list for your form fields. Another frequent challenge is handling potentially malicious input. You should always sanitize user input to prevent vulnerabilities like Cross-Site Scripting (XSS) attacks (OWASP, 2021). While Flask-WTF provides some built-in protection against XSS, it's crucial to be aware of potential risks and sanitize data before displaying it or storing it in the database. This might involve escaping HTML characters or using a templating engine that automatically escapes data by default. By implementing robust server-side input validation, you protect your application from invalid data, prevent vulnerabilities, and ensure data integrity. This is a fundamental best practice for any web application.

7.2 Error handling: Implementing proper error handling and displaying user-friendly error messages.

Proper error handling is paramount for creating robust and user-friendly web applications. Imagine a scenario where a user is attempting to purchase an item on an e-commerce site. A sudden network hiccup disrupts the connection to the payment gateway. Without proper error handling, the application might crash, display a cryptic error message, or worse, silently fail, leaving the user unsure whether their order was processed. For Computer Engineering students and educators, mastering error handling techniques is critical for building reliable and maintainable systems. Effective error handling involves anticipating potential points of failure, gracefully catching exceptions, meticulously logging errors for debugging, and presenting informative yet user-friendly messages.

The process begins by identifying potential points of failure. These might include database interactions, file operations, network requests, or any code susceptible to exceptions. Encapsulate these potentially problematic code sections within try...except blocks. For example: try: result = payment_gateway.process_payment(order) except PaymentGatewayError as e: logging.error(f"Payment gateway error: {e}"); flash('There was a problem processing your payment. Please try again later.', 'danger'); return render_template('checkout.html', error="Payment failed"). This code attempts to process a payment. If a

PaymentGatewayError occurs, the code within the except block executes. Crucially, the error is logged using logging.error() for later debugging. A user-friendly message is displayed using flash(), and the user is redirected or the current page is re-rendered with an error message. A frequent question is: "Why not display the raw error message directly to the user?" Displaying raw error messages can expose sensitive system information and confuse non-technical users. Generic, user-friendly messages are preferable for public display, while detailed error logs are essential for developers.

Another key aspect is providing context-specific error messages. Instead of generic messages like "An error occurred," provide more targeted information when possible, without revealing sensitive details. For instance, if a user enters an invalid credit card number, a message like "Invalid credit card number. Please check your input." is more helpful. A common question is: "How do I handle various exception types?" Multiple except blocks can handle different exceptions: try: ... except PaymentGatewayError as e: ... except InvalidCreditCardError as e: ... except DatabaseError as e: ... except Exception as e: .... This granular approach allows for tailored error handling for each specific exception type. A frequent challenge is handling HTTP errors like 404 (Not Found) or 500 (Internal Server Error). Flask provides mechanisms for handling these gracefully. Custom error handlers can be defined using the @app.errorhandler() decorator: @app.errorhandler(404) def page_not_found(e): return render_template('404.html'), 404. This renders a custom 404 page. Robust error handling is crucial for creating stable and user-friendly applications. It ensures that the application doesn't crash unexpectedly and provides users with helpful feedback, even when things go wrong. Thorough error logging is also vital for diagnosing and resolving issues during development and in production.

7.3 Security best practices: Protecting your application from common vulnerabilities (e.g., SQL injection).

Security best practices are paramount in web application development. Imagine you're building a banking application. A seemingly small vulnerability, like a SQL injection flaw, could allow an attacker to steal sensitive financial data, manipulate accounts, or even take down the entire system. For Computer Engineering students and educators, understanding and implementing security best practices is not just good practice—it's a professional imperative. Protecting your application from common vulnerabilities like SQL injection, Cross-Site Scripting (XSS), and Cross-Site Request Forgery (CSRF)1 is crucial for maintaining data integrity, user trust, and the overall security of your system. Let's focus on SQL injection as a prime example.

SQL injection vulnerabilities arise when user-supplied input is directly incorporated into SQL queries. Attackers can craft malicious input that alters the intended query, allowing them to execute arbitrary SQL code. A classic example is a login form that's vulnerable to SQL injection. If the code constructs a query like this: SELECT * FROM users WHERE username = '" + username + "' AND password = '" + password + "'", an attacker could enter a username like ' OR '1'='1 and a password like ' OR '1'='1. This would modify the query to SELECT * FROM users WHERE username = '' OR '1'='1' AND password = '' OR '1'='1', effectively bypassing authentication. A frequent question is: "How can I prevent SQL injection?" The most effective way is to *never* directly concatenate user input into SQL queries. Instead, use parameterized queries or prepared statements. Parameterized queries treat user input as data, not as executable code. They separate the SQL code from the data, preventing the attacker from injecting malicious SQL.

In a Flask application using SQLAlchemy, you should *always* use SQLAlchemy's query API, which automatically parameterizes queries. For example, instead of User.query.filter(User.username == username).first(), which is vulnerable if username comes directly from user input, you would use User.query.filter_by(username=username).first(). filter_by is safe from SQL injection. If you need more complex queries, use the filter method with proper parameterization: User.query.filter(User.username == bindparam('username')).params(username=username).first(). The bindparam and params methods ensure that the username is treated as a parameter, not as part of the SQL code. A common question is: "Are ORMs like SQLAlchemy sufficient to prevent SQL injection?" Yes, when used correctly, ORMs like SQLAlchemy provide built-in protection against SQL injection. However, it's crucial to use the ORM's query API and avoid writing raw SQL queries whenever possible. If you absolutely must use raw SQL, use parameterized queries or prepared statements. Another frequent concern is: "What about other vulnerabilities like XSS and CSRF?" XSS vulnerabilities occur when malicious JavaScript is injected into a web page, allowing attackers to steal cookies, hijack sessions, or deface websites. Proper output encoding and input sanitization are essential for preventing XSS. CSRF vulnerabilities allow attackers to trick users into performing unwanted actions on a website. CSRF tokens, which are unique, unpredictable values included in forms, are used to prevent CSRF attacks. Flask-WTF provides built-in CSRF protection. By understanding and addressing these common vulnerabilities, you can significantly improve the security of your web application and protect it from a wide range of attacks. Regular security audits and penetration testing are also recommended to identify and address potential vulnerabilities.

7.4 Using Bootstrap for styling: Styling your forms and pages using Bootstrap CSS.

Using Bootstrap for styling is a highly effective way to rapidly develop visually appealing and responsive web applications. Imagine you're building a web application for managing a university's student clubs. You need a consistent and professional look across all pages, from the club registration form to the event calendar and the member directory. Bootstrap, a popular CSS framework, provides a collection of pre-styled components, a responsive grid system, and a wealth of utility classes that simplify the styling process. For Computer Engineering students and educators, understanding how to leverage Bootstrap is invaluable for creating modern and maintainable user interfaces. Bootstrap saves you from writing extensive CSS from scratch and ensures a consistent design across your application.

The process begins by including Bootstrap's CSS and JavaScript files in your HTML templates. You can either download these files and host them yourself or use a Content Delivery Network (CDN). Using a CDN is often preferred for production environments as it leverages the CDN's caching infrastructure, potentially leading to faster loading times for your users. Bootstrap's website provides CDN links that you can directly include in your HTML. In your Jinja2 templates, you would include the CSS file in the <head> section: <link rel="stylesheet" href="https://cdn.jsdelivr.net/npm/bootstrap@5.3.0/dist/css/bootstrap.min.css"> (replace with the current Bootstrap version). You'll typically also want to include the Bootstrap JavaScript bundle just before the closing </body> tag: <script src="https://cdn.jsdelivr.net/npm/bootstrap@5.3.0/dist/js/bootstrap.bundle.min.js"></script>.1 A frequent question is: "Why include the JavaScript bundle?" Bootstrap's JavaScript components, such as dropdowns, modals, and tooltips, rely on this JavaScript. If you're using these components, you'll need to include the bundle.

Once Bootstrap is included, you can start using its classes and components to style your forms and pages. For example, to style a form, you can wrap the form elements in Bootstrap's form groups and use classes like form-label, form-control, and btn. A simple form example: <form> <div class="mb-3"> <label for="username" class="form-label">Username</label> <input type="text" class="form-control" id="username"> </div> <button type="submit" class="btn btn-primary">Submit</button> </form>. This will style the form elements with Bootstrap's default form styling. A common question is: "How do I customize Bootstrap's styling?" You can customize Bootstrap's styling in several ways. You can override the default styles by writing your own CSS rules in a separate stylesheet. You can also use Bootstrap's theming capabilities to customize the color scheme and other visual aspects. Bootstrap also provides utility classes for common styling tasks, such as margins, padding, colors, and display properties. These utility classes can save you a lot of time and effort. For example, mt-3 adds a top margin of 1rem (16px) to an element.

Another frequent question is: "How do I use Bootstrap's grid system?" Bootstrap's grid system is based on rows and columns. You can use the row class to create a row and the col-* classes to define the width of columns within that row. For example: <div class="row"> <div class="col-md-6">Column 1</div> <div class="col-md-6">Column 2</div> </div>. This will create two columns that each take up half the width of the row on medium-sized screens and larger. The responsive grid system allows you to create layouts that adapt to different screen sizes. By using Bootstrap effectively, you can quickly create professional-looking and responsive web applications without having to write a lot of custom CSS. This is a valuable skill for any web developer.

7.5 Refactoring and code organization: Improving the structure and readability of your code.

Refactoring and code organization are essential practices for maintaining and scaling web applications. Imagine you're working on a web application that has grown significantly over time. The codebase has become tangled, difficult to understand, and prone to bugs. Making even small changes can introduce unexpected issues. For Computer Engineering students and educators, understanding and applying refactoring and code organization principles is crucial for building maintainable, scalable, and collaborative projects. Refactoring involves improving the internal structure of your code without changing its external behavior. Code organization focuses on arranging your code in a logical and consistent manner.

One of the first steps in refactoring is identifying code smells. Code smells are indicators of potential problems in your code, such as duplicate code, long methods, large classes, or excessive comments. Addressing these code smells can significantly improve the readability and maintainability of your code. A common code smell is duplicate code. If you find yourself repeating the same code logic in multiple places, you should extract it into a separate function or method. This not only reduces code duplication but also makes it easier to maintain the code, as you only need to make changes in one place. Another frequent code smell is long methods. Methods that are too long can be difficult to understand and debug. You should break down long methods into smaller, more manageable methods, each with a specific purpose. A frequent question is: "How long should a method be?" There's no strict rule, but generally, methods should be short and focused, ideally performing a single logical operation.

Code organization involves arranging your code in a logical and consistent way. This includes using meaningful names for variables, functions, and classes, following consistent coding conventions, and organizing your code into modules or packages. Using meaningful names makes your code easier to understand. Instead of using names like x or temp, use names that describe the purpose of the variable or function. For example, instead of x, use user_age or total_price. Following consistent coding conventions (e.g., PEP 8 for Python) makes your code look uniform and easier to read. Organizing your code into modules or packages helps to manage complexity and makes it easier to find and reuse code. A common question is: "How should I organize my Flask application?" For larger Flask applications, consider using blueprints to organize your code into logical units. Each blueprint can represent a specific part of your application, such as user authentication, data management, or API endpoints.

Refactoring and code organization are ongoing processes. You should refactor your code regularly, not just when it becomes a mess. Small, frequent refactoring is much easier than large, infrequent refactoring. A good practice is to refactor your code after you've finished implementing a new feature or fixing a bug. This helps to keep your code clean and maintainable. Another frequent challenge is deciding when to refactor. A good rule of thumb is to refactor whenever you see a code smell, whenever you need to make a change to the code, or whenever you feel that the code is becoming difficult to understand. By consistently applying refactoring and code organization principles, you can create a codebase that is easier to understand, maintain, and extend, ultimately leading to higher quality software.

7.6 Testing your application (unit tests, integration tests).

Testing is an indispensable part of the software development lifecycle. Imagine you're developing a complex e-commerce platform. Without thorough testing, you risk deploying code with hidden bugs that could lead to lost sales, corrupted data, or even security breaches. For Computer Engineering students and educators, understanding and implementing various testing strategies is crucial for building reliable and high-quality applications. Testing helps to identify and fix bugs early in the development process, reduces the cost of maintenance, and increases confidence in the software's quality. There are different types of testing, each serving a specific purpose. We'll focus on unit tests and integration tests.

Unit tests focus on testing individual units of code, such as functions, methods, or classes. The goal is to isolate each unit and verify that it behaves as expected. Imagine you have a function that calculates the total price of items in a shopping cart. A unit test for this function would involve calling the function with various inputs (e.g., different quantities, different prices) and asserting that the function returns the correct total price for each input. Python's unittest module or the pytest framework are commonly used for writing unit tests. A frequent question is: "How do I write effective unit tests?" Unit tests should be small, focused, and easy to understand. They should cover all possible code paths and edge cases. A good practice is to write unit tests *before* you write the code being tested (Test-Driven Development or TDD). This helps you to think about the design of your code and ensures that it is testable.

Integration tests, on the other hand, test the interaction between different units of code or different components of your application. They verify that these units work together correctly. For example, an integration test might test the entire process of adding an item to a shopping cart, from clicking the "Add to Cart" button to updating the cart total and displaying it on the page. Integration tests often involve interacting with external resources, such as databases or APIs. A common question is: "How do I test interactions with a database?" You can use test databases or mocks to isolate your tests from the actual database. A test database is a separate database that you use only for testing. Mocks are objects that simulate the behavior of real objects, allowing you to control the responses of external resources in your tests. Frameworks like Flask-Testing or Selenium can be used for writing integration tests for web applications.

Another frequent concern is: "How much testing is enough?" There's no easy answer, but you should aim for high test coverage, meaning that your tests cover a large percentage of your code. However, test coverage is not the only metric to consider. It's also important to test critical parts of your application thoroughly and to consider edge cases and boundary conditions. A good practice is to have a combination of unit tests and integration tests. Unit tests help to catch bugs early in the development process, while integration tests ensure that the different parts of your application work together correctly. By implementing a comprehensive testing strategy, you can significantly improve the quality and reliability of your web applications. This is a fundamental best practice for any software development project.

Example Project Ideas

- **Simple To-Do List:** A classic CRUD example.

- **Product Catalog:** Good for practicing more complex data relationships.

- **Blog:** Involves text editing and potentially user authentication.

- **Library Management System:** A more challenging project that can incorporate more advanced features.

Bibliography

[1] Python Software Foundation. (n.d.). *Python.org*.

[2] Python Packaging Authority. (n.d.). *venv - Creating Virtual Environments*.

[3] Stonebraker, M., & Kemnitz, G. (1995). *The Ingres Papers: Anatomy of a Relational Database System*. Addison-Wesley.

[4] Grinberg, M. (2018). *Flask Web Development: Developing Python Web Applications*. O'Reilly Media.

[5] Python Packaging Authority. (n.d.). *The Python Packaging Guide*.

[6] Gray, J. (1978). *Operating systems: An advanced course*. Springer-Verlag.

[7] Flask-WTF Documentation.

[8] OWASP. (2021). *SQL Injection Prevention Cheat Sheet*.

[9] OWASP. (2021). *Cross-Site Request Forgery (CSRF)*.

[10] OWASP. (2021). *Cross-Site Scripting (XSS) Prevention Cheat Sheet*

About The Author

Mark John Lado is an accomplished Information System Specialist with a strong background in education and technology. He holds a Master's degree in Information Technology from Northern Negros State College of Science and Technology and is currently pursuing his Doctorate in the same field.

Mark boasts a diverse professional experience, having served as an ICT Instructor/Coordinator at Carmen Christian School Inc., a Part-time Information Technology Instructor at the University of the Visayas, and a Faculty member at Colegio de San Antonio de Padua and Cebu Technological University. He is currently a Faculty member at the College of Technology and Engineering at Cebu Technological University.

His expertise extends beyond the classroom, encompassing Object-Oriented Programming, Teacher Mentoring, Computer Hardware, Software System Analysis, and Web Development. He actively participates in the Philippine Society of Information Technology Educators (PSITE) as a member and has contributed to the academic community through the publication of his research article, "A Wireless Digital Public Address with Voice Alarm and Text-to-speech Feature for Different Campuses," in Globus An International Journal of Management & IT.

Mark's dedication to education and passion for technology are evident in his contributions to various educational institutions, including Cebu Technological University, University of the Visayas - Danao Campus,

Colegio de San Antonio de Padua, and Carmen Christian School Inc.

Biography Source:

Mark John Lado. (n.d.). *Biographies.net.* Retrieved January 24, 2025, from https://www.biographies.net/

Authors' Official Website:
https://markjohnlado.com/